13

The Phallic Quest

Marie-Louise von Franz, Honorary Patron

**Studies in Jungian Psychology
by Jungian Analysts**

Daryl Sharp, General Editor

The Phallic Quest

Priapus and Masculine Inflation

JAMES WYLY

For Mary

Canadian Cataloguing in Publication Data

Wyly, James, 1937-
  The phallic quest: Priapus and masculine inflation

(Studies in Jungian psychology by Jungian analysts; 38)

Bibliography: p.
Includes index.

ISBN 0-919123-37-6

1. Penis—Psychological aspects.   2. Masculinity (Psychology).
3. Men—Psychology.   4. Priapus (Greek deity).   5. Jung, C.G.
(Carl Gustav), 1875-1961.   I. Title.   II. Series.

BF692.5.W94 1989   155.3'32   C89-093807-5

INNER CITY BOOKS
Box 1271, Station Q, Toronto, Canada M4T 2P4
Telephone (416) 927-0355

Honorary Patron: Marie-Louise von Franz.
Publisher and General Editor: Daryl Sharp.
Senior Editor: Victoria Cowan.
Editorial Board: Fraser Boa, Daryl Sharp, Marion Woodman.
Production: David Sharp.

INNER CITY BOOKS was founded in 1980 to promote the
understanding and practical application of the work of C.G. Jung.

Front Cover: Terracotta drinking-bowl mask, from Pompeii, 1st
century A.D. (National Museum, Naples).

Back Cover: Priapic Mercury, wall painting, possibly from
Pompeii, reign of Nero (National Museum, Naples).

Index by Daryl Sharp.

Printed and bound in Canada by Webcom Limited

Contents

See final pages for descriptions of other Inner City Books

Illustration Credits

Pages 13, 23, 33, 35, 38, 91, 103, 110, 117, courtesy of the Newberry Library of Chicago.

Pages 11, 20, 30, 43, 44, 45, 46, 47, 48, 52, 72, 94, 96, from *Eros in Antiquity*, photographs by Antonio Mulas, The Erotic Art Book Society, New York, 1978.

Pages 27, 115, from C.G. Jung, *Symbols of Transformation*, CW 5.

Pages 55, 98, from Joseph Campbell, *The Mythic Image* (Bollingen Series C), Princeton University Press, Princeton, 1974.

Page 59, from Michael Stapleton, *A Dictionary of Greek and Roman Mythology*, New York, Bell Publishing Company, 1978.

Page 66, from Stanislas K. de Rola, *Alchemy: The Secret Art*, Avon Books, New York, 1973.

Acknowledgments

As this book has moved toward completion, I have realized more and more the magnitude of the debt I owe to my analysands, particularly those who consented to having their dream material appear in it. The interchange that daily takes place between us is responsible for whatever insights this work may contain.

I am also deeply grateful to Joseph Pasic for the knowledge, enthusiasm and many discussions with which he furthered the preparation of the manuscript. The original idea came from an inspired remark of Thomas Lavin's; without it, the book would simply not have been.

Finally, I thank the Newberry Library of Chicago for permission to use many of the illustrations that complement the text.

An inflated consciousness is always egocentric and conscious of nothing but its own existence. . . . It is hypnotized by itself and therefore cannot be argued with. It inevitably dooms itself to calamities that must strike it dead.
—C.G. Jung, *Psychology and Alchemy.*

Men who resist serious reflection on the pomposity and inflation of patriarchal assumptions of supremacy are priapic psychologically.
—Eugene Monick, *Phallos: Sacred Image of the Masculine.*

Terracotta drinking-bowl mask.
(1st cent. A.D., from Pompeii; National Museum, Naples).

Introduction

In the process of putting up some window blinds, a middle-aged man stepped onto a window sill and became aware that he could stand erect within the frame of a window which he had carefully measured and found to be 66 inches, or 5'6", high. This was a rather unsettling surprise, for since adolescence the man had believed himself to be 68 inches tall.

In trying to understand how he could have misperceived his own stature for more than thirty years, the man remembered how he had arrived at the inflated figure. As an adolescent he had simply compared himself to the two men he knew best: his grandfather, than whom he was a shade taller and who was said to be 5'7", and his father, than whom he was slightly shorter, and who claimed he was 5'9" tall.

Since the differences in height were probably accurate, the window frame demonstrated an inflation of two inches or so in all the figures. Not only had this man gone through his adult life believing he was two inches taller than he was; his father and grandfather had apparently done the same thing.

On reflection, we can see that all three of these men grew up with their culture's assumption that the taller, bigger, heavier and stronger a man is, the more masculinity he somehow possesses. If this assumption can lead to ignorance of something as fundamental and personal as one's own height, we may well wonder what else in our collective culture has been distorted due to this apparent need to inflate the nature and dimensions of the masculine. The disturbing preoccupation of modern men with more and more power, limitless competition, *machismo* and violence suggests itself as one significant result of this inflationary process.

Yet the swollen, "inflated" phallus is the physiological instrument of male creativity. As such, it has provided a metaphor for masculinity for as long as humankind has been capable of metaphor. Inflation is a process essential to masculine functioning, not an inherently pathological phenomenon. Therefore, its inseparability from that which we identify as masculine contributes to the ease with which contemporary men succumb to its destructive side. *Phallos* is the name employed by Eugene Monick and others for the elaboration of this concept, and Monick's discussion of it demonstrates its inseparability from the achievement of creative autonomy by men.[1]

Having said this, our concern here will be primarily with inflation's destructive aspect. To demonstrate the etiology of destructive masculine inflation and to suggest an attitude with potential for transcending it are the purposes of this book.

In order to do this, I shall have to move freely between the realms of physiology and imagination, of fact and metaphor, and of psychology and mythology, working on the assumption that behind them all lies an archetypal ground, to which all else acts as metaphor, and which can only be known through the images it presents. Empirical material, represented on the collective level by myths and cultural phenomena and on the individual level by dreams of contemporary men in analysis, will provide the images upon which my argument is based.

The archetype in question appears in classical culture in the figure of Priapus, the god with enormous genitals. His emergence and a culture's perception of a need to deal with him are the phenomena delimiting this study.

Priapus was a relative latecomer to the classical religious awareness; it is only from around Augustan times that extensive evidence of his cult survives from ancient Rome, and he was not recognized in the Greek states until the time of the Macedonian domination.[2] This must mean there was some kind of shift in classical psycho-religious awareness which created a need for that which had not been needed before: a god-image with an unrealistically large phallus.

---

[1] See *Phallos: Sacred Image of the Masculine.*

[2] Edward Trip, *The Meridian Handbook of Classical Mythology,* p. 497.

A supplicant at the temple of Priapus.
(from Mons St. Evremont, *The Satyrical Works of Titus Petronius Arbiter*, 1708)

If we can equate the appearance of a god-image with a coming-to-consciousness of some psychic content which has the capability of being separated or split off, then we are in a position to appreciate such an appearance as symbolic of a shift in the way a culture receives the archetypal ground upon which it stands. Classical culture at that point needed Priapus to reintegrate a part of masculinity which had become split off from it.

Now if splitting off of unconscious contents results in their potential for autonomous action in the world, as Jungian psychology demonstrates to be the case,[3] then the splitting off of the inflationary-creative aspect of the masculine would result in its acting autonomously until it brought itself to the attention of consciousness. We shall need to be careful here, remembering that we are not discussing a suppression of the masculine as a whole, but a suppressed awareness of a specific part of it. The result can be envisioned as a psychological distortion in which masculinity's phallic aspect is separated from its whole. The part remaining in consciousness necessarily expands, that is becomes inflated. But it is nevertheless a fragment, and a distortion of the masculine whole. The hypocritical inflation of some Christian priests' vows, with their arbitrary and unsuccessful denial of sexual imperatives, provides a good example of this process.

Now we could say that inflation and masculinity are inseparable. But inflation is properly a characteristic of the phallic, and there it is creative. When the phallic is split off and inaccessible, inflation happens to that which remains; and this is the dangerous inflation which is our subject.

When it is split off, the priapic complex can be expected to demand reintegration. It does this by puncturing the inflated ego position that seems to accompany the split. This happens in individuals

---

[3] See Jung's empirical data establishing the existence and autonomy of psychological complexes, especially "Studies in Word Association" in *Experimental Researches,* CW 2. (CW refers throughout to *The Collected Works of C.G. Jung)*

just as it happens in cultures. The discovery of an inflation of two inches in his height was impossible for the man I mentioned above to ignore; and, on a cultural level, *phallos* will present itself in the form of a divinity that demands reintegration, as did Priapus.

I intend to suggest that the destructive psychological inflation which is my concern here is a result of a modern-day, culture-wide splitting off of this priapic archetype and its resultant demand for attention and conscious reintegration; that something similar happened in classical times; and that classical mythology can provide us with metaphors which, if we elaborate them with depth psychology, will show us ways to deal with this very dangerous happening, both in the culture and in the individual.

*

It will be helpful to define a couple of terms at the outset. Our subject is inflation, and we must be clear about what it means. Jung most often refers to the ego-inflation that is the inevitable result of ego's assimilation of unconscious contents:

> To annex the deeper layers of the unconscious, which I have called the *collective unconscious,* produces an enlargement of the personality leading to the state of inflation. This state is reached by simply continuing the analytical work . . . . By continuing the analysis we add to the personal consciousness certain fundamental, general, and impersonal characteristics of humanity, thereby bringing about the inflation I have just described, which might be regarded as one of the unpleasant consequences of becoming fully conscious.[4]

Or again:

> The great psychic danger which is always connected with individuation, or the development of the self, lies in the identification of ego consciousness with the self. This produces an inflation which threatens ego-consciousness with dissolution.[5]

---

[4] *Two Essays on Analytical Psychology,* CW 7, par. 243.
[5] "Concerning Rebirth," *The Archetypes and the Collective Unconscious,* CW 9i, par. 254.

In *Aion* and elsewhere, Jung calls this kind of inflation a result of the ego's assimilation by the Self.[6] This is *not* the kind of inflation I shall discuss in this book. Rather, my concern is with the inflation that Jung says results from the opposite process, the assimilation of the Self by the ego. Jung describes it:

> Although this is the exact opposite of the process we have just described it is followed by the same result: inflation. The world of consciousness must now be levelled down in favour of the reality of the unconscious. In the first case, reality has to be protected against an archaic, "eternal" and "ubiquitous" dream-state: in the second, room must be made for the dream at the expense of the world of consciousness. In the first case, mobilization of all the virtues is indicated; in the second, the presumption of the ego can only be damped down by moral defeat. This is necessary, because otherwise one will never attain that median degree of modesty which is essential for the maintenance of a balanced state. It is not a question, as one might think, of relaxing morality itself but of making a moral effort in a different direction. For instance, a man who is not conscientious enough has to make a moral effort in order to come up to the mark, while for one who is sufficiently rooted in the world through his own efforts it is no small moral achievement to inflict defeat on his virtues by loosening his ties with the world and reducing his adaptive performance.[7]

Therefore, when I say inflation I mean an enlargement of the ego that results from ego's assumption of functions of the Self unless I qualify the term otherwise.

An example of this kind of inflation can be seen in the kind of ego-psychology that assumes ego can set goals and control life, regardless of unconscious processes. The reverse, Jung's first kind, would be the abandonment of ego to the unconscious in the kind of grandiose religious enslavement often found among devoted members of so-called religious cults.

The other term about which we must be clear is *phallos*. In general, by *phallos* I mean all that to which the symbol of the phallus refers. Jung regards it as fundamentally a symbol for libido: "A

---

[6] "The Self," *Aion,* CW 9ii, par. 45.
[7] Ibid., par. 47.

phallic symbol," he writes, "does not denote the sexual organ, but the libido, and however clearly it appears as such, it does not mean *itself* but is always a symbol of the libido."[8]

Libido energizes and enlivens, as the sperm does the ovum; and that which it energizes is its psychological opposite: the mother potential, the matrix. As Jung points out,

> "Mother" is an archetype and refers to the place of origin, to nature . . . . It also means the unconscious, our natural and instinctive life, the physiological realm, the body in which we dwell or are contained; for the "mother" is also the matrix, the hollow form, the vessel that carries and nourishes, and it thus stands psychologically for the foundations of consciousness."[9]

By *phallos*, then, I mean the energy with which one mobilizes individuality, which exists in the psyche as a matrix, a "hollow form," in order to differentiate one's self from the collective. It is by no means unique to men; arguably, the function of the animus or inner man in women, as Jung conceived it, can closely parallel the function of *phallos* we are examining. But here I am speaking of men. *Phallos* is the energy with which a man creates, and although in creating he makes nothing new, he nevertheless enlivens that which is implicit in the cosmos, or the psyche.

This energy is represented mythically by Zeus's thunderbolt, or Eros's arrows, or Aaron's rod. With it, man's first creation is necessarily an awareness of himself (always potentially there, but initially unknown to consciousness) which can withstand the assaults and projections of the surrounding environment without resorting to grandiose and unrealistic postures—that is to say, without resorting to inflation.

---

[8] *Symbols of Transformation,* CW 5, par. 329.
[9] "The Practical Use of Dream-Analysis," *The Practice of Psychotherapy,* CW 16, par. 344.

Part One
The Background

Priapus weighing himself.
(House of the Vettii, Pompeii, 1st cent. A.D.)

1

The Mythology of Priapus

Our starting point will be the stories of Priapus which were current in classical Greece and Rome from roughly the second century B.C. to the fourth century A.D. The stories themselves are scattered and few; but they contain themes and allusions which lead out in all directions, into the complex web of classical mythology. Tracing these threads provides a rich texture of additional stories. Later we shall encounter these elaborations again, when we consider inflation as it is found in clinical material and in cultural phenomena.

Priapus was held by Pausanius to be the child of Dionysus and Aphrodite,[1] though Adonis, Hermes and Pan have been mentioned as his father and Chione as his mother.[2] Hera, either out of jealousy of Aphrodite or outrage at her promiscuity, caused him to be born with enormous genitals. A pot belly and other exaggerations are also sometimes encountered. His mother abandoned him, and he was reared by shepherds.[3]

In two stories, Priapus is associated with the ass. First, Robert Graves cites Ovid's account of Priapus's attempt, while drunk, to violate Hestia "at a rustic feast attended by the gods, when everyone had fallen asleep from repletion; but an ass brayed aloud, Hestia awoke, screamed to find Priapus about to straddle her, and sent him running off in comic terror."[4]

Edward Trip cites Hyginus's account of the other. Priapus got into an argument with an ass to which Dionysus had given a human voice. Writes Trip:

---

[1] Pausanius, *Guide to Greece,* vol. 1, p. 374.
[2] *Larousse Encyclopedia of Mythology,* p. 183.
[3] C. Kerényi, *The Gods of the Greeks,* p. 176.
[4] *The Greek Myths,* vol. 1, pp. 74-75.

The full story is only hinted at, but it may be guessed that Priapus and the ass, a beast noted for erotic prowess, were debating the relative sizes of the physical appendages of which they were most proud. The boasting led to a contest in which the god came off the worse. Enraged at this defeat, Priapus beat the ass to death with a stick. Dionysus immortalized the ass by placing him in heaven as one of the two stars called the Asses.[5]

Kerényi tells us that Priapus seems eventually to have found some favor with Hera, for she made him Ares' dancing instructor.[6]

Priapus's image was commonly set up in gardens and orchards, where he "presides over the fecundity of fields and flocks, over the raising of bees, the culture of the vine, and over fishing."[7] In Funk and Wagnall's we read that "his sacrifice is the first fruits of the farm."[8] Graves further writes that "he is a gardener, and carries a pruning knife,"[9] and is known as "pruner of the pear-tree"[10]—which is sacred to Hera.

Priapus's huge penis naturally provides us with the focal point for a psychological elaboration of these stories. Also, its size means we shall need to consider the implications of phallic exaggeration. But there are several other themes implied in these stories, and each develops as a metaphor which will prove most important when we later come to translate the myths into psychological language.

We can start with the implications of Priapus's parentage. It would take a major digression to develop fully the theme of Dionysus as a father, but the connection to the ecstatic, the instinctual, dancing, the vine, nature and Pan—as opposed to that side of masculinity represented by Apollo: reason, deliberation, discipline and so on—should be clear enough without one. Priapus is born of instinctual physical

---

[5] *The Meridian Handbook of Classical Mythology,* p. 497.

[6] *The Gods of the Greeks,* p. 176.

[7] *Larousse Encyclopedia of Mythology,* p. 184.

[8] *Funk & Wagnall's Standard Dictionary of Folklore, Mythology and Legend,* p. 886.

[9] *The Greek Myths,* vol. 1, p. 69.

[10] Ibid., vol. 2, p. 406.

Aphrodite and Adonis.
(from Ovid, *Les Metamorphoses,* trans. l'Abbé Banier, 1732)

ecstasy and, on his mother's side, of sexuality; for as Graves tells us, Aphrodite's sole divine duty was to make love.[11]

If we consider that in addition to Dionysus, Adonis and Hermes were sometimes said to be Priapus's father, we can see something else: that Priapus tends to be a product of a beautiful, adolescent, even effeminate-appearing masculinity, as though his huge genitals compensate the nascent masculinity with which Aphrodite became infatuated in his father. Hera's function in "deforming" Priapus would then seem to be an attempt to restore some kind of balance in Aphrodite's affections—just as Hera's acts so often turn out to contain compensating maneuvers behind the superficial jealous retribution.

Given Priapus's heritage, one can understand why it is Hestia, of all the goddesses, whom he tries to violate. Hestia is the self-effacing, virgin ruler of the hearth and domesticity. In a sense, it is the security of domesticity that Priapus's childhood abandonment by his mother denied him. His mother, the ultimate seductress, can have found it no easier to succeed in a maternal role than do many such women today; and it is to be expected that, like anyone who experiences abandonment, Priapus felt rage at his loss.

Furthermore, as a child of the dionysian and the aphrodisiac, Priapus represents a union of two forces that are notoriously disruptive to domestic stability when they demand integration into a seemingly established life or relationship.

But why is the animal that betrays him in his violation—his attempt for recognition, one could say—an ass, his traditional associate?

I think a series of associations in Graves explains this, for it leads to the theme of castration, which, as the opposite of the priapic and as a concretization of the splitting off of the phallic, is implied in our entire study. The wild ass, Graves tells us, is the spirit of the desert wind, the sirocco, known as " 'the breath of the Wild Ass, or Typhon' . . . which brings bad dreams, and murderous inclinations,

---

11 Ibid., vol. 1, p. 70.

and rapes."[12] He further tells us that "the god Set, whose breath Typhon [the sirocco] was said to be, maimed Osiris."[13] And Osiris's dismemberment, of course, resulted in the permanent loss of his penis, the only one of the fourteen fragments into which he was cut that the goddess Isis was unable to recover.

This is not the only mythic road from Priapus to castration. Another, as might be guessed, is to be found in his designation as "pruner of the pear-tree." Again, to cite Graves, phallic images sacred to Priapus were often wooden columns—that is, trees: "The pear-tree was sacred to Hera as prime goddess of the Peloponnese, which was therefore called Apia,"[14] and "the most ancient image of the Death-goddess Hera, in the Heraeum at Mycenae, was made of pear-wood."[15]

Graves also tells us that "Apis is the noun formed from *apios,* a homeric adjective usually meaning 'far off' but, when applied to the Peloponnese (Aeschylus: Suppliants 262), 'of the pear-tree.'"[16] But *apis* is Latin for bee; and, to the Latin mind, the Peloponnese, Hera's place, was inevitably associated with bees, of which Hera therefore became the queen.

There were rites of Cybele which were widely practiced in the Rome of the first centuries A.D. The Romans considered Cybele to be the wife of Saturn, who castrated Uranos, and her rites derived from Aphrodite Urania's destruction of the sacred king,

> who mated with her on a mountain top, as a queen bee destroys the drone: by tearing out his sexual organs. Hence . . . the worship of Cybele, the Phrygian Aphrodite of Mount Ida [and equivalent to the hermaphrodite Agdistis], as a queen bee, and the ecstatic self-castration of her priests in memory of her lover Attis.[17]

---

12 Ibid., p. 133.

13 Ibid., p. 135.

14 Ibid., p. 71.

15 Ibid., p. 252.

16 Ibid., p. 211.

17 Ibid., p. 71.

Castration, then, is never far from Priapus, and his pruning-knife takes on a potential use which we shall need to bear in mind. Furthermore, the Attis theme of self-castration as a result of love-gone-mad for a hermaphroditic mother/lover has implications which deserve development in connection with some forms of contemporary homosexuality and their fascination with phallic imagery. (It is an interesting point that the blood from Attis's wound became violets, which first grew beneath the pine tree where he wounded himself,[18] for their color has a long-standing association with these homosexual modes.)

Now, to complete this chain of mythological association we must add material on the theme of the tree, already mentioned in the contexts of Priapus's wooden phallic images and of the pear-tree he prunes. Having also established an association with the Great Mother Cybele, we can use the following passage from Jung to pull together and elaborate this part of our material:

> Another equally common mother-symbol is the wood of life . . . or tree of life. The tree of life may have been, in the first instance, a fruit-bearing genealogical tree, and hence a kind of tribal mother. Numerous myths say that human beings came from trees, and many of them tell how the hero was enclosed in the maternal tree trunk, like the dead Osiris in the cedar-tree, Adonis in the myrtle, etc. Numerous female deities were worshipped in tree form, and this led to the cult of sacred groves and trees. Hence when Attis castrates himself under a pine-tree, he did so because the tree has a maternal significance. Juno of Thespiae was a bough, Juno of Samos a plank, Juno of Argos a pillar, the Carian Diana was an unhewn block of wood, Athene of Lindus a polished column. Tertullian called the Ceres of Pharos "rudis palus et informe lignum sine effigie" (a rough and shapeless wooden stake with no face). Athenaeus remarks that the Latona at Delos was . . . "an amorphous bit of wood." Tertullian also describes an Attic Pallas as a "crucis stipes" (cross-post). The naked wooden pole, as the name itself indicates . . . is phallic.[19]

---

18 Kerényi, *The Gods of the Greeks,* p. 90.
19 *Symbols of Transformation,* CW 5, par. 321.

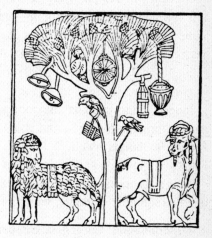

The sacred tree of Attis.
(relief from an altar to Cybele)

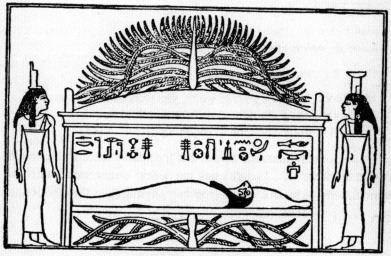

Osiris in the cedar coffin.
(relief, Dendara, Egypt)

Jung goes on to point out that the Greek word *phallós* could des-
ignate "a pole, a ceremonial lingam carved out of figwood," that Roman statues of Priapus were of figwood, and that *phallós* and *pha-
lanx*—which means finger-joint—have a common root.[20] Finger-
joints lead to castration as well as phallic autonomy, for when Attis's
mother/lover begged Zeus to make Attis live again, all Zeus would
enliven was Attis's smallest finger-joint, which continued to move of
its own accord.[21]

Indeed, Jung extends the root *phal* to *phalós*—which he says
means "bright, shining"—and notes that "the Indo-European root is
*bhale, 'to bulge, swell.' " "Who," asks Jung, "does not think of
Faust's 'It glows, it shines, increases in my hand!' "[22]

Jung's associative tour-de-force amplifies the surrounding context
of Faust's double-entendre, which Jung quotes elsewhere:

Mephistopheles: Congratulations, before you part from me!
You know the devil, that is plain to see.
Here, take this key.

Faust: That little thing! But why?
Mephistopheles: First grasp it; it is nothing to decry.

Faust: It glows, it shines, increases in my hand!

Mephistopheles: How great its worth, you soon shall understand.
The key will smell the right place from all others:
Follow it down, it leads you to the Mothers![23]

To Jung, the implication here is that the phallic leads to the "realm
of the mothers . . . [which] has not a few connections with the
womb, with the matrix, which frequently symbolizes the creative aspect of the unconscious."[24]

---

20 Ibid.
21 Kerényi, *The Gods of the Greeks,* p. 90.
22 *Symbols of Transformation,* CW 5, par. 321.
23 Ibid., par. 180.
24 Ibid., par. 182.

In making this last observation, Jung has done what our mythological exposition did in different metaphors, which is to demonstrate that a right relationship to *phallos* seems to lead to a *coniunctio,* a creative encounter between *phallos* and the matrix, between masculine and feminine.

Separation from *phallos*—in effect, castration—results in sterility, and in a fascination with the phallus which is bent on its recovery. But the search naturally inflates the importance of the searched-for object; and should the searcher lack psychological awareness and confuse the concrete symbol with the goal, his search will become the perpetual, fruitless phallic quest which brings many men into analysis.

Priapus pouring.
(bronze sculpture, 1st cent. A.D.; National Museum, Naples)

2
Priapus in Classical Literature

The mythology surrounding Priapus makes it appear that he *is* the split-off *phallos*. This separation is the result of a union between the feminine (Aphrodite, Cybele, Agdistis) and an adolescent or effeminate masculine (Dionysus, Adonis, Attis) which cannot bring fully developed phallic power into their relationship.[1] This particular masculine-feminine union, then, castrates; that is, it suppresses *phallos*. *Phallos* then takes on an autonomous life of its own as the complex symbolized by Priapus with his enormous penis.

If Priapus is a god who takes form when attention is focused on a relatively non-phallic masculine, then he is a compensatory phenomenon; and, as he is both divine and an exaggeration, he carries his own countercompensation, the knife that can prune the tree back to a healthy size. Thus there is a balance inherent in the figure of Priapus.

But mortals are not like gods, and do not have automatic access to successfully compensatory mechanisms. Human compensation tends to run to the opposite extreme, rather than maintain a balance. (It might even be argued that this lack of automatic balancing is the chief thing that distinguishes the gods from mortals!) For mortals, compensation seems to work successfully only when it is recognized by consciousness. This requires insight and an effort of will. The making conscious of psychologically compensatory images is, of course, what Jungian analysis aims to do.

Therefore, we cannot expect a culture or an individual to move on from a priapic mode—that is, a masculinity in which phallic potency is consciously undervalued and unconsciously deified—to a new

---

[1] The exaggeratedly underendowed male statuary of classical times may be a manifestation of just this male ideal in late Hellenic and Roman esthetics.

balance. Rather, it—or he, or even she[2]—will veer from extreme to extreme, alternating phases of dangerous inflation with phases of murderously excessive pruning—meanwhile remaining covertly fascinated with the denied, the phallic, in whatever forms it tries to present itself for reintegration.

Our next task, then, will be to describe parallels to this mythic/psychological situation in examples drawn first from literature and then from contemporary medical and psychological material.

Three documents from the period of approximately 100 B.C. to 200 A.D. deserve our attention: Petronius's *Satyricon*, Apuleius's *The Golden Ass*, and a collection of mostly anonymous Latin poetry known as the *Priapeia*, or *Carmina Priapeia*. We shall consider them in this order.

The *Satyricon* needs to be treated with caution, both because it exists only in fragmentary form and because its satirical nature makes it difficult, at this distance, to form solid conclusions about what one encounters in it. But the basic plot-line still demonstrates a phallic quest of exactly the type suggested by the mythic material cited in chapter one.

The hero, Encolpius (which means, roughly, "the crotch"[3]), is on an odyssey of excess that is a conscious parody of Homer's original. Clearly, he is inflated: he has a grandiose view of himself as lover, rake and con man. His lifestyle is an offense to Priapus, who makes him impotent, thus endangering Encolpius's view of himself and his relationship to his lover Giton.

Giton is a slave who is described at one point as "a boy, approximately sixteen, curly-haired, attractive, effeminate."[4] He represents

---

[2] Just as men have no monopoly on the power drive, so they are not alone in being susceptible to inflation. In Jungian terminology, priapic inflation in a woman would be described as a characteristic of her animus.

[3] Petronius, *The Satyricon*, p. xii.

[4] Ibid., p. 102. It is important to note that Giton's being male does not mean he or Encolpius is homosexual in anything like the modern sense. Both relate to both sexes in about the same spirit as twentieth-century Don Juans move from blondes to brunettes and back.

Encolpius and Giton.
(from Petronius, *A Revised Latin Text of the Satyricon*,
illus. Norman Lindsay, 1890)

the kind of masculinity regarded by most of the book's characters, whether male or female, as immensely attractive. Here, then, is a fixation on the kind of masculinity that fathers—that is, splits off—Priapus. The split, as pointed out earlier, causes inflation of that which remains.

Encolpius tries every cure for his recurring impotence but one—sacrifice of his grandiosity. Naturally, nothing works. The resulting phallic quest provides the framework for all the novel's action. Petronius's psychological point seems to be that when there is no authentic relationship to *phallos,* inflation is the way masculinity takes to give itself meaning. He found numerous examples of inflation around him and exploited them fully in satirizing his culture. The excesses of Trimalchio's household and the terrible poetry of Encolpius's traveling companion, Eumolpus, are two of many examples.

At a banquet so long that the invitations were for two days instead of a specified hour, Trimalchio speaks of his possessions in language familiar to us all:

> But silver's my real passion. I've got a hundred bowls that hold three or four gallons apiece, all of them with the story of Cassandra engraved on them: how she killed her sons, you know, and the kids are lying there dead so naturally that you'd think they were still alive. And there's a thousand goblets too which Mummius left my old master. There's pictures on them too, things like Daedalus locking up Niobe in the Trojan Horse. And on my cups, the heavy ones, I've got the fights of Hermeros and Petraites. No sir, I wouldn't take cash down for my taste in silver.[5]

And an excerpt from Eumolpus's "The Fall of Troy" will demonstrate the extent to which he inflates his metaphors:

> Then lo, Apollo spoke, and Ida's wooded flanks were felled, the forest seaward dragged, and the tall trees chopped and shaped to make a horse of war, a giant hulk, within whose mass a cavelike hole was hollowed out.

---

[5] Ibid., p. 59.

The inflated Eumolpus.
(from Petronius, *A Revised Latin Text of the Satyricon*,
illus. Norman Lindsay, 1890)

Here in the caverned void, the chafing host was hid, ten long and weary years of soldier bravery confined, ambushed in their gift to god.[6]

Meanwhile, of course, the search for *phallos* continues. Encolpius travels from place to place and quack to quack in his effort to restore his potency. The astonishing thing here is that Priapus never relents. In the end, it is Hermes who makes Encolpius potent again.

We must reserve discussion of this important point until more material has been presented; but for now, we can note that Encolpius's long and fruitless pursuit of Priapus is not unlike the long and similarly fruitless pursuits of a sense of masculine effectiveness carried out nightly in late-twentieth-century bars.

*

Before elaborating upon why Priapus does not restore that which he takes away, we will examine our other documents. *The Golden Ass* seems to present the same kind of quest, but here it is clothed quite differently.

We know little of Apuleius's life; but we know enough to be able to suggest that it also involves the young and beautiful man/mature woman relationship that gives birth to Priapus and necessitates this phallic quest. Apuleius, a blond, fair and therefore rather exotic North African, married a woman in her forties when he was about twenty-nine. In her interpretation of the story, Marie-Louise von Franz suggests that Apuleius had a positive mother complex:

He was one of those men who evaded an ultimate fight with his mother to free his masculinity. By escaping into homosexuality and into an intellectual way of living,[7] in a way eliminating the feminine principle, the man of concrete enterprise in him did not get into

---

6 Ibid., pp. 93-94.

7 Some homosexual poetry by Apuleius survives. I am not sure his culture would have regarded homosexuality, as it was apparently practiced then, in the same light as von Franz does.

life, did not fight the fight against the mother principle. In this novel he catches up.[8]

Apuleius's hero, Lucius, is introduced as a rather inflated young man who seduces a notorious witch's maid, Fotis, and persuades her to let him watch as her mistress, Pamphilë, magically turns herself into an owl. Naturally, he wants to try the same charm, but when he does there is a mixup and he becomes an ass instead.

Lucius's forms, before and after the transformation, show us exactly the adolescent Dionysus/Priapus split. When Lucius meets his old nursemaid, Byrrhaena, before the change, she recognizes him because of his resemblance to his mother, Salvia:

Salvia had exactly the same slenderness and upright carriage, the same rosy cheeks and delicate skin, the same yellow hair neatly dressed, the same alert, shining grey eyes that used to remind me of an eagle's, the same graceful way of walking.[9]

But when he is transformed, the priapic is the center of attention:

The hair on [my arms] grew coarser and coarser and the skin toughened into hide. Next, my fingers bunched together into a hard lump so that my hands became hooves, the same changes came over my feet, and I felt a long tail sprouting from the base of my spine. Then my face swelled, my mouth widened, my nostrils dilated, my lips hung flabbily down, and my ears shot up long and hairy. The only consoling part of this miserable transformation was the enormous increase in the size of a certain organ of mine; because I was by this time finding it increasingly difficult to meet all Fotis's demands upon it.[10]

In this humiliating form he has a series of fantastic, frequently sexual adventures. It seems to follow that Lucius as the ass represents the psychologically split-off phallic energy of Apuleius's narrative persona, and that the novel itself is the quest for reunion. Again, this is *not* accomplished by the phallic god himself, but in this

---

[8] *A Psychological Interpretation of the Golden Ass of Apuleius,* p. 20.
[9] Apuleius, *The Golden Ass,* p. 26.
[10] Ibid., p. 71.

Lucius watches as Pamphilë turns herself into an owl.
(from Apuleius, *Les Metamorphoses ou l'Asne dor,* 1648)

case by the goddess Isis, to whom Lucius eventually devotes himself. Thus, the phallic quest becomes a kind of unconscious subplot to Lucius's conscious quest for magical power—which is to say, a quest for ego-satisfaction through inflation.

We can never know how much of this Apuleius was conscious of as he wrote, or where in his own psycho-religious journey (he was himself initiated into a number of mystery cults) he was when he wrote it. But the phallic quest of a man initially stuck in psychological adolescence clearly emerges as the psychological underpinning of the work.

*

"The Priapeia is a collection of Latin epigrams and poems relating to Priapus, compiled by an unknown editor who apparently wrote the first, introductory poem," writes an early translator, Mitchell S. Buck.[11] The remainder of his short introduction follows, for it describes this rather obscure collection well.

> It is uncertain how many of the poems were in circulation. A good many, undoubtedly, were found attached to, or inscribed on, statues of the god. A few are out of place by subject and are probably careless additions of a later date. III is by Ovid, LXXXII and LXXXIII by Tibullus and the last three are ascribed variously to Virgil or Catullus; but the authors of the others are unknown.
>
> While lacking the austerity of the earlier Greek works, they still present Priapus as a patron of gardens, generally, but not necessarily, a rural divinity. The statues to which they refer were usually of wood, with a terminal base similar to that of the hermae. It is not unlikely that, in addition to their general significance, they often served the same purpose as a "scarecrow" and, possibly, as a rack for the farmers' scythe.
>
> The primary purpose of the statue or altar amidst fruits and vegetables was, of course, to bring the blessing of Priapus's attribute of fecundity to these growing things. This attribute, which with his definite connection with the principle of generation, had found him a

---

[11] *The Priapeia,* Introduction (pages unnumbered).

place in most of the Greek Mysteries, was literally indicated by the presence of a greatly exaggerated phallus. It was inevitable that, in the later period, this "corporal mark" should provoke amusement and references to it as a weapon for the punishment of thieves, a theme running throughout this anthology. There is, in most of the poems, a noticeable absence of divination of anything but the obvious.

The character of this humor, as will be noted, is distinctly male and Rabelaisian, and it runs the gamut of irony and satire, unabashed. In this sphere, particularly, the Priapeia is a classic source of considerable importance.[12]

Until very recently, the *Priapeia* was quite inaccessible. Buck's English translation, made in 1937, was privately printed in an edition of 150 copies. Now W.H. Parker's thoroughly scholarly edition of 1988 makes available both the Latin texts and Parker's new translations.[13]

Parker's versions differ radically from Buck's, and neither makes the psychologically oriented reader's task easy; for the "laconic elegance of the original," to which one reviewer of Parker's translations refers,[14] appears to be irretrievably lost among the crude associations that are inseparable from the English language's sexual vocabulary. This means that the conscientious reader has to proceed very carefully. Nevertheless, the poems provide valuable material for understanding the place Priapus held in classical Roman culture.

Two poems from the *Priapeia* follow. The first is in Parker's translation, the second in Buck's.

Hey, you, who the temptation can hardly withstand
Upon our rich orchard to lay a deft hand:
This watchman'll go in and out your back door
With gusto until you can't stand any more;
Two more will come afterwards, from either side,
With beautiful penises richly supplied,
And they'll set to work, and dig deeper in;

---

12 Ibid.

13 *Priapeia: Poems for a Phallic God.*

14 Hugh Lloyd-Jones, "Members Only," in *The New York Review,* Nov. 10, 1988, p. 23.

An ass with huge member on you'll then begin.
It surely makes sense not to play any tricks,
When it means being punished by so many pricks![15]

This stupid mentule does not grow in length
As once it did, nor stand with proper strength,
Although by hands assisted. Woe is me.
For passionate girls, 'tis a catastrophe
Of tiny uselessness. This strange new shame
And damage will disgust them with my game.
Of much more use, Tydeus was, if Homer's tale is true,
Who, small in body, had a nature nothing could subdue.[16]

The attitude toward Priapus which emerges here is constant throughout the collection, and can be assumed to have been general in Roman culture of that time. Priapus makes nature produce when sacrifices are made to him, but when he is not so honored, he withdraws. Barren fields, stolen crops and impotence can result, and Priapus threatens rape. Furthermore, Priapus is honored in specific ways: by putting up and maintaining herm-like images and by making sacrifices near them.

The point here is that these are conscious acts of sacrifice to a concrete phallic image, far different from the ribald and fruitless phallic quests of Encolpius and Lucius, in which simple recognition of and respect for the phallic image itself are rationalized and exploited in countless ego-gratifying ways. Indeed, the sacrificial attitude is considerably nearer the kind of conscious awareness of psychological facts fostered by contemporary Jungian analysis than is the attitude of twentieth-century ego-inflation.[17]

---

[15] *Priapeia,* trans. Parker, p. 151.

[16] *Priapeia,* trans. Buck, No. LXXX (pages unnumbered).

[17] The attitude of making sacrifices to a phallic god-image is, of course, pervasive in oriental religions. Christianity made every effort to eradicate it in Europe, but apparently it persisted nearly until modern times in some remote places. Sir William Hamilton observed such rites, evidently intended to restore or increase male potency, in Isernia, near Naples, in 1780. His description of them was published by Richard Payne Knight (*A Discourse on the Worship of Priapus*). Neither Knight nor Wright, who published a sup-

The same attitude is apparent in the phallic ornamentation and statuary discovered in the ruins of Pompeii and Herculaneum. Examples of this extraordinary artwork appear on the following pages and elsewhere in this book. Such images have been cited as evidence of licentiousness or carnality in Roman culture of the first century A.D. But if they are results of the attitude toward the phallic found in the *Priapeia* (and why should they not be?), it is not so much carnality as awareness of a psychological truth toward which they are striving. (This would mean that some present-day assumptions about the sexual attitudes of classical Rome may simply be projections of that which our culture would rather not see in itself.)

*

Now we are in a position to address the question of why Priapus seems not to give back what he takes away—that is, he does not restore what he prunes. If we follow the trail backward to his parents, we can see that for Priapus to restore potency would be in effect to restore unconsciousness—the mother-fixated adolescent's unconsciousness of his own phallic potential and completion.

The desire for this pleasant state of youthful, unpunctured inflation—a happily potent Encolpius, or a Lucius convinced that he can be superhuman through magic—is understandable, and is repeated whenever an analysand expresses the wish that therapy restore a former happiness which was based on an inflated ego-position. But this is impossible, just as to intentionally restore a state of unconsciousness is impossible. The deflationary wounds that brought the

---

plemental essay to Knight's in the 1865 edition, appears to have perceived any connection between Priapus and psychological inflation.

Hermann Rorschach interviewed members of a Swiss phallus-worshipping cult in 1913. He never completed his study. The surviving fragments (in *Gesammelte Aufsätze,* untranslated) are summarized by Henri Ellenberger in his article "The Life and Work of Hermann Rorschach." It appears that what Rorschach found was quite far, in its religious function, from the kind of sacrifice to Priapus we are here discussing.

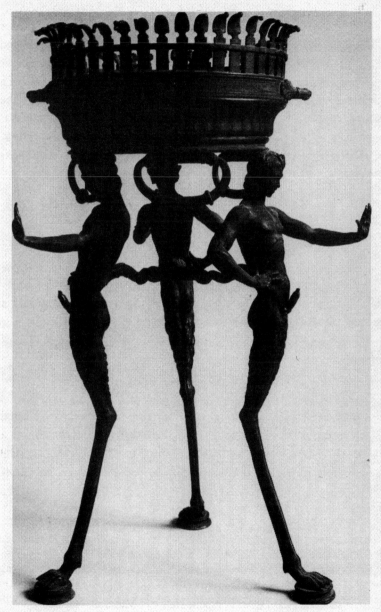

Bronze tripod with ithyphallic young Pans.
(1st cent. A.D., from Pompeii; National Museum, Naples)

Terracotta lamp in the shape of a faun.
(1st cent. A.D., from Pompeii; National Museum, Naples)

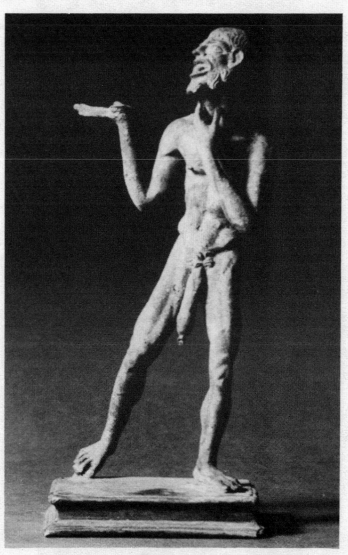

Placentarius.
(gilded bronze, 1st cent. A.D., from Pompeii;
National Museum, Naples)

Morio, drilopus in terracotta.
(1st cent. A.D., from Herculaneum; National Museum, Naples)

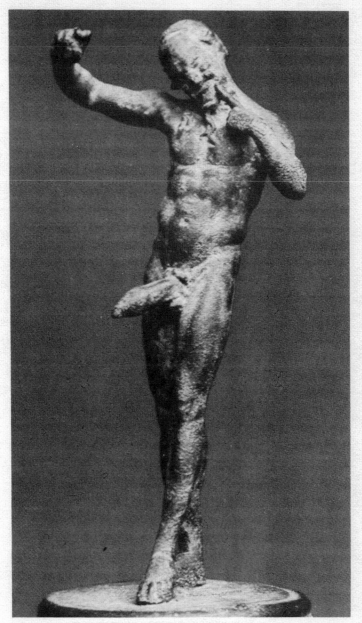

Bronze dancer.
(1st cent. B.C., from Civita; National Museum, Naples)

The pollyphallus, bronze tintinnabulum.
(1st cent. B.C., from Herculaneum; National Museum, Naples)

person into analysis cannot be made to go away, for they are the re-sult of an encounter with reality.

A new reality requires a new, more conscious adaptation, which means the resources of other divinities will be required. In other words, the phallic quest seems to be a quest for the restoration of un-consciousness, and so is doomed from the beginning. Analysis must lead to its abandonment, so that "other gods"—hitherto unconscious potentialities—can come into play and a new adaptation to the reali-ties of life can be made.

It must be in this way that we are to understand the restoration scene at the end of the *Satyricon*. The text seems especially frag-mented here, so the scene lacks context. Nevertheless, what happens is clear:

> "There are other gods still more powerful," I [Encolpius] explained, "and it is they who have made me a man once more. Mercury him-self, the god who guides our unborn souls to the light and leads the dead to hell, has taken pity on me and given me back that power which an angry hand once cut away. Look at me and tell me whether Protesilaus or any of those ancient heroes was ever more blessed by heaven than I am now."
>
> With that, I lifted my tunic and displayed myself in my erected glory. Gaping with astonishment and awe, utterly incapable of be-lieving his eyes, he reached out his shaking hands and caressed that huge pledge of heaven's favor.[18]

Obviously Encolpius is anything but modest about his recovery; and if this scene follows the pattern of everything else we know about Priapus, Encolpius has set himself up for still another en-counter with his god.

Lucius's restoration in *The Golden Ass* is more fully described. In the form of an ass, he naturally suffers the equivalent of a humiliating and extended loss of person. He is mistreated in every possible way and must watch helplessly as others are mistreated. At first he in-wardly bewails his fate, but gradually he accepts it and so becomes a

---

[18] Petronius, *The Satyricon*, p. 163.

better ass, and then a rather ingenious one, at which point he is treated more humanely.

Eventually Lucius has a dream of Isis, who tells him to be at a procession that is to be held in her honor. A priest in the procession, who has had parallel dreams, knows to feed the ass the roses that will turn him back into Lucius.

But it is not the Lucius of before. Now he is required to be initiated as a priest of Isis, which involves financial sacrifices and a rigorous lifestyle very different from his former one. The priest of Isis explains to him:

> Lucius, my friend, you have endured and performed many labors and withstood the buffetings of all the winds of ill luck. Now at last you have put into the harbor of peace and stand before the altar of loving-kindness. Neither your noble blood and rank nor your education sufficed to keep you from falling a slave to pleasure; youthful follies ran away with you. Your luckless curiosity earned you a sinister punishment. But blind Fortune, after tossing you maliciously about from peril to peril has somehow, without thinking what she was doing, landed you here in religious felicity. . . . She has no power to hurt those who devote their lives to the honor and service of our Goddess's majesty. . . . But to secure today's gains, you must enroll yourself in this holy Order as last night you pledged yourself to do, voluntarily undertaking the duties to which your oath binds you; for her service is perfect freedom.[19]

This would seem to reinforce Goethe's and Jung's point referred to in chapter one, that a conscious relationship with *phallos* leads to a creative union with the impersonal feminine—a *coniunctio* that is transformative, seen in the dream of Isis that leads to the ass's transfiguration. The creative potential of this union leads Lucius to two more religious initiations, further psycho-religious transformations, and even success in the world, for he eventually opens a lucrative legal practice in Rome.[20]

---

[19] Apuleius, *The Golden Ass*, pp. 272-273.
[20] Ibid., pp. 273ff.

It is safe to assume that the attitude of consciousness of the phallic, seen in the *Priapeia* and dictated by surroundings which include phallic poetry, images, carvings and sacrifices on every hand, would lead in the same direction; for it is, after all, awareness and acceptance of his priapic form that opens Lucius to the transformative encounter with Isis.

The moment we speak of this kind of masculine/feminine relationship, a creative union, we are speaking of the archetype of the parental couple. Conscious submission to the priapic by the formerly inflated youth, then, transforms him in the sense that it makes him able to function creatively, as a father.

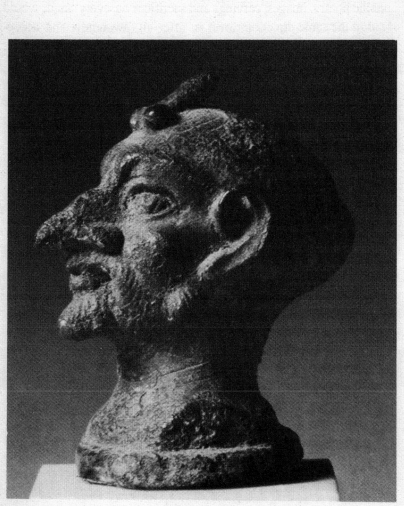

Bronze sculpture
(from the Borgia Museum; National Museum, Naples)

3
Priapus in a Twentieth-Century Story

One more literary work must be considered, for it will help us to move our mythic material from classical times to our own. I am referring to Thomas Mann's *Death in Venice*. I shall quote substantially from it in this chapter, for in it we can find the myth of the birth of Priapus transported intact into early twentieth-century Europe. But in a twentieth-century setting the outcome is different.

Unlike Lucius and (presumably) Encolpius, Mann's hero, Gustave von Aschenbach, receives no gesture of restoration of *phallos*. There must be something in his situation or attitude, then, that prevents the Priapus myth from reaching its intended resolution; and we need to consider what that may be if we are to say something useful for twentieth-century men who are caught in this complex.

When we meet Aschenbach, he is described as having always encountered some difficulty in living up to his reputation:

Aschenbach's whole soul, from the very beginning, was bent on fame—and thus, while not precisely precocious, yet thanks to the unmistakable trenchancy of his personal accent he was early ripe and ready for a career. Almost before he was out of high school he had a name. Ten years later he had learned to sit at his desk and sustain and live up to his growing reputation, to write gracious and pregnant phrases in letters that must needs be brief, for many claims press upon the solid and successful man. At forty, worn down by the strains and stresses of his actual task, he had to deal with a daily post heavy with tributes from his own and foreign countries.

Remote on one hand from the banal, on the other from the eccentric, his genius was calculated to win at once the adhesion of the general public and the admiration, both sympathetic and stimulating, of the connoisseur. From childhood up he was pushed on every side to achievement, and achievement of no ordinary kind; and so his young days never knew the sweet idleness and blithe *laissez aller* that belong to youth. A nice observer once said of him in company—it was at the time when he fell ill in Vienna in his thirty-fifth year:

"You see, Aschenbach has always lived like this"—here the speaker closed the fingers of his left hand to a fist—"never like this"—and he let his open hand hang relaxed from the back of his chair. It was apt. And this attitude was the more morally valiant in that Aschenbach was not by nature robust—he was only called to the constant tension of his career, not actually born to it.[1]

This is a state of inflation, of course; it is that inflated identification with an ego-constructed persona image which is still endemic in our culture. We can expect, then, that there is a dissociation of *phallos*, and that *phallos* may present itself to Aschenbach's psyche in an obsession which will demand reintegration at the sacrifice of the persona image. This is the modern equivalent to the sacrifices offered to Priapus in classical times, apparently in order to prevent just such a disaster as befalls Aschenbach.

Aschenbach goes to Venice, where he encounters Tadzio. It may seem an improbably long road from the ecstatic god who fathers Priapus to the angelic fourteen-year-old Tadzio; but, just as Dionysus, kidnapped by pirates who took him for a helpless boy, drove his captors to madness and destruction,[2] so Tadzio kills—or (for this is the twentieth century) Aschenbach's obsession with him does.

Again we find the theme of fascination for the beautiful adolescent which seems essential to the birth of Priapus; but in Aschenbach's culture, in contrast to the classical, such a fascination was totally inadmissible, and that much more dangerous.

Mann was aware of the mythic parallels his material evokes. The first time Aschenbach sees Tadzio, there are clear erotic overtones in the way the boy's relationship to his mother, sisters and governess is described. These recall Dionysus's affair with Aphrodite:

Round a wicker table next him was gathered a group of young folk in charge of a governess or companion—three young girls, perhaps fifteen to seventeen years old, and a long-haired boy of about fourteen. Aschenbach noticed with astonishment the lad's perfect beauty. His face recalled the noblest moment of Greek sculpture—pale, with

---

[1] *Death in Venice*, p. 9.
[2] Robert Graves, *The Greek Myths*, vol. 1, p. 106.

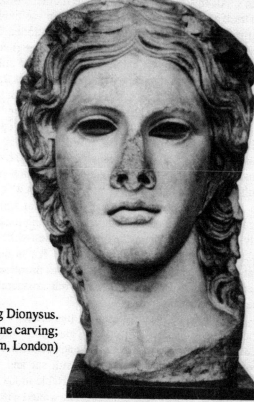

Head of the young Dionysus.
(late Hellenistic stone carving;
British Museum, London)

a sweet reserve, with clustering honey-coloured ringlets, the brow and nose descending in one line, the winning mouth, the expression of pure and godlike serenity. Yet with all this chaste perfection of form it was of such unique personal charm that the observer thought he had never seen, either in nature or art, anything so utterly happy and consummate. What struck him further was the strange contrast the group afforded, a difference in educational method, so to speak, shown in the way the brother and sisters were clothed and treated. The girls, the eldest of whom was practically grown up, were dressed with an almost disfiguring austerity. All three wore half-length slate-coloured frocks of cloister-like plainness, arbitrarily unbecoming in cut, with white turn-over collars as their only adornment. Every grace of outline was wilfully suppressed; their hair lay smoothly plastered to their heads, giving them a vacant expression, like a nun's. All this could only be by the mother's orders; but there was no trace of the same pedagogic severity in the case of the boy. Tenderness and softness, it was plain, conditioned his existence. No scissors had been put to the lovely hair that (like the Spinnario's) curled about his brows, above his ears, longer still in the neck. He wore an English sailor suit, with quilted sleeves that narrowed round the delicate wrists of his long and slender though still childish hands. And this suit, with its breastknot, lacing, and embroideries, lent the slight figure something "rich and strange," a spoilt, exquisite air. The observer saw him in half profile, with one foot in its black patent leather advanced, one elbow resting on the arm of his basket-chair, the cheek nestled into the closed hand in a pose of easy grace, quite unlike the stiff subservient mien which was evidently habitual to his sisters. Was he delicate? His facial tint was ivory-white against the golden darkness of his clustering locks. Or was he simply a pampered darling, the object of a self-willed and partial love? Aschenbach inclined to think the latter. For in almost every artist's nature is inborn a wanton and treacherous proneness to side with the beauty that breaks hearts, to single out aristocratic pretensions and pay them homage.

A waiter announced, in English, that dinner was served. Gradually the company dispersed through the glass doors into the dining-room. Latecomers entered from the vestibule or the lifts. Inside, dinner was being served; but the young Poles still sat and waited about their wicker table. Aschenbach felt comfortable in his deep arm-chair, he enjoyed the beauty before his eyes, he waited with them.

The governess, a short, stout, red-faced person, at length gave the signal. With lifted brows she pushed back her chair and made a bow to the tall woman, dressed in palest gray, who now entered the hall. This lady's abundant jewels were pearls, her manner was cool and measured; the fashion of her gown and the arrangement of her lightly powdered hair had the simplicity prescribed in certain circles whose piety and aristocracy are equally marked. She might have been, in Germany, the wife of some high official. But there was something faintly fabulous, after all, in her appearance, though lent it solely by the pearls she wore: they were well-nigh priceless, and consisted of earrings and a three-stranded necklace, very long, with gems the size of cherries.[3]

---

[3] *Death in Venice*, pp. 25-27.

When we recall that Dionysus had long hair and was brought up as a girl, and that in classical times the pearl was the gem associated above all others with Aphrodite, any lingering doubts we may have about Mann's intent to draw this mythical analogy are dispelled.

Mann evokes other mythical adolescents. To Aschenbach, Tadzio's was "the head of Eros, with the yellowish bloom of Parian marble, with fine serious brows, and dusky clustering ringlets standing out in soft plenteousness over temples and ears!"[4] Aschenbach becomes obsessed with the beautiful boy, but effective action is utterly unimaginable to him and he is reduced to a paralyzing, compulsive voyeurism. This is in direct contrast to classical attitudes toward similar obsessions, as Mann reminds us by comparing Tadzio to Ganymede:

> He [Aschenbach] would write, and moreover he would write in Tadzio's presence. This lad should be in a sense his model, his style should follow the lines of the figure that seemed to him divine; he would snatch up this beauty into the realms of the mind, as once the eagle bore the Trojan shepherd aloft. Never had the pride of the word been so sweet to him, never had he known so well that Eros is in the word, as in those perilous and precious hours when he sat at his rude table, within the shade of his awning, his idol full in his view and the music of his voice in his ears, and fashioned his little essay after the model Tadzio's beauty set: that page and a half of choicest prose, so chaste, so lofty, so poignant with feeling, which would shortly be the wonder and admiration of the multitude. Verily it is well for the world that it sees only the beauty of the completed work and not its origins nor the conditions whence it sprang; since knowledge of the artist's inspiration might often but confuse and alarm and so prevent the full effect of its excellence. Strange hours, indeed, these were, and strangely unnerving the labour that filled them! Strangely fruitful intercourse this, between one body and another mind! When Aschenbach put aside his work and left the beach he felt exhausted, he felt broken—conscience reproached him, as it were after a debauch.[5]

---

4 Ibid., p. 29.
5 Ibid., pp. 46-47.

Here we encounter the difference between Aschenbach's time and classical culture. When Zeus in the guise of an eagle bore Ganymede aloft to be cupbearer to the gods, the young boy "rejoiced the eye of all by his beauty."[6] But Aschenbach cannot experience adolescent masculine beauty without an overwhelming sense of guilt that poisons his effort. Perhaps this is why his mythic analogy turns from Zeus's successful abduction of Ganymede to Apollo's infatuation with Hyacinthus, which ended in disaster when the jealous Zephyrus killed the youth with an "errant" discus:

> When the sun was going down behind Venice, he would sometimes sit on a bench in the park and watch Tadzio, white-clad, with gay-coloured sash, at play there on the rolled gravel with his ball; and at such times it was not Tadzio whom he saw, but Hyacinthus, doomed to die because two gods were rivals for his love. Ah, yes, he tasted the envious pangs that Zephyr knew when his rival, bow and cithara, oracle and all forgot, played with the beauteous youth; he watched the discus, guided by torturing jealousy, strike the beloved head; paled as he received the broken body in his arms, and saw the flower spring up, watered by that sweet blood and signed forevermore with his lament.[7]

So Aschenbach remains unable to assimilate his obsession. He is struck impotent because he has not honored or acted upon the phallic component of his masculinity, living instead an inflated life bound by that which ego finds acceptable.

Aschenbach's secret, kept even from himself, is Priapus; and his attitude toward his personal secret is shown by Mann's equation of it with Venice's collective secret, a deadly outbreak of Asiatic cholera:

> Thus did the fond man's folly condition his thoughts; thus did he seek to hold his dignity upright in his own eyes. And all the while he kept doggedly on the traces of the disreputable secret the city kept hidden at its heart, just as he kept his own—and all that he learned fed his passion with vague, lawless hopes. He turned over newspapers at cafes, bent on finding a report on the progress of the disease; and in the German sheets, which had ceased to appear on the hotel

6 *Larousse Encyclopedia of Mythology,* p. 138.

7 Ibid., pp. 49-50.

Roman mosaic of Ganymede, the Trojan prince, being carried off by Zeus in the form of an eagle.

table, he found a series of contradictory statements. The deaths, it was variously asserted, ran to twenty, to forty, to a hundred or more; yet in the next day's issue the existence of the pestilence was, if not roundly denied, reported as a matter of a few sporadic cases such as might be brought into a seaport town. After that the warnings would break out again, and the protests against the unscrupulous game the authorities were playing. No definite information was to be had.[8]

In the face of this conscious attitude, we would expect that phallic power would surface in Aschenbach's dreams; and this is exactly what happens. The electrifying dream, cited below, is preceded in the novel by several allusions to dionysian abandon. It is as though Mann is preparing us for the encounter of the adolescent Dionysus-image with its priapic offspring, which encounter is the inevitable result of Aschenbach's growing obsession with Tadzio.

Aschenbach follows Tadzio and his sisters through Venice:

> Once he lost them from view, hunted feverishly over bridges and in filthy *culs-de-sac,* only to confront them suddenly in a narrow passage whence there was no escape, and experience a moment of panic fear. Yet it would be untrue to say he suffered. Mind and heart were drunk with passion, his footsteps guided by the daemonic power whose pastime it is to trample on human reason and dignity.[9]

Street musicians come to the hotel and perform a song with a refrain which "was nothing but rhythmical, unmodulated laughter,"[10] which naturally becomes contagious and involves the listeners.

Aschenbach gets a clerk in the English travel bureau to tell him the truth about the cholera. The disease, he finds, has brought about increased intemperance, indecency and crime:

> Evenings one saw many drunken people, which was unusual. Gangs of men in surly mood made the streets unsafe, theft and assault were said to be frequent, even murder; for in two cases persons supposedly victims of the plague were proved to have been poisoned by their own families. And professional vice was rampant, displaying ex-

---

[8] Ibid., p. 57.
[9] Ibid., p. 55.
[10] Ibid., p. 61.

cesses heretofore unknown and only at home much farther south and in the east.[11]

Thus the stage is set for Aschenbach's dream, which might be described as compensation with a vengeance.

That night he had a fearful dream—if dream be the right word for a mental and physical experience which did indeed befall him in deep sleep, as a thing quite apart and real to his senses, yet without his seeing himself as present in it. Rather its theatre seemed to be his own soul, and the events burst in from the outside, violently overcoming the profound resistance of his spirit; passed him through and left him, left the whole cultural structure of a lifetime trampled on, ravaged, and destroyed.

The beginning was fear; fear and desire, with a shuddering curiosity. Night reigned, and his senses were on the alert; he heard loud, confused noises from far away, clamor and hubbub. There was a rattling, a crashing, a low dull thunder; shrill halloos and a kind of howl with a long-drawn *u*-sound at the end. And with all these, dominating them all, flute-notes of the cruellest sweetness, deep and cooing, keeping shamelessly on until the listener felt his very entrails bewitched. He heard a voice, naming, though darkly, that which was to come: "The stranger god!" A glow lighted up the surrounding mist and by it he recognized a mountain scene like that about his country home. From the wooded heights, from among the tree-trunks and crumbling moss-covered rocks, a troop came tumbling and raging down, a whirling rout of men and animals, and overflowed the hillside with flames and human forms, with clamour and the reeling dance. The females stumbled over the long, hairy pelts that dangled from their girdles; with heads flung back they uttered loud hoarse cries and shook their tambourines high in the air; brandished naked daggers or torches vomiting trails of sparks. They shrieked, holding their breasts in both hands; coiling snakes with quivering tongues they clutched about their waists. Horned and hairy males, girt about the loins with hides, drooped heads and lifted arms and thighs in unison, as they beat on brazen vessels that gave out droning thunder, or thumped madly on drums. There were troops of beardless youths armed with garlanded staves; these ran after goats and thrust their staves against the creatures' flanks, then clung to the

---

[11] *Ibid.*, p. 65.

plunging horns and let themselves be borne off with triumphant shouts. And one and all the mad rout yelled that cry, composed of soft consonants with a long-drawn *u*-sound at the end, so sweet and wild it was together, and like nothing ever heard before! It would ring through the air like the bellow of a challenging stag, and be given back many-tongued; or they would use it to goad each other on to dance with wild excess of tossing limbs—they never let it die. But the deep, beguiling notes of the flute wove in and out and over all. Beguiling too it was to him who struggled in the grip of these sights and sounds, shamelessly awaiting the coming feast and the uttermost surrender. He trembled, he shrank, his will was steadfast to preserve and uphold his own god against this stranger who was sworn enemy to dignity and self-control. But the mountain wall took up the noise and howling and gave it back manifold; it rose high, swelled to a madness that carried him away. His senses reeled in the steam of panting bodies, the acrid stench from the goats, the odour as of stagnant waters—and another, too familiar smell—of wounds, uncleanness, and disease. His heart throbbed to the drums, his brain reeled, a blind rage seized him, a whirling lust, he craved with all his soul to join the ring that formed about the obscene symbol of the godhead, which they were unveiling and elevating, monstrous and wooden, while from full throats they yelled their rallying-cry. Foam dripped from their lips, they drove each other on with lewd gesturings and beckoning hands. They laughed, they howled, they thrust their pointed staves into each other's flesh and licked the blood as it ran down. But now the dreamer was in them and of them, the stranger god was his own. Yes, it was he who was flinging himself upon the animals, who bit and tore and swallowed smoking gobbets of flesh—while on the trampled moss there now began the rites in honour of the god, an orgy of promiscuous embraces--and in his very soul he tasted the bestial degradation of his fall.[12]

Given the opening of the dream, we might expect Dionysus to be "the stranger god"; but there is no need for Dionysus to appear in Aschenbach's dreaming, for he is already in his awareness, in the form of Tadzio. But this is the late classical adolescent Dionysus, and the dream tries to restore the priapic energy that is split off from him. The "stranger god" is he who is represented by a wooden phallus.

---

[12] Ibid., pp. 66-68.

Aschenbach's dream confronts him with images of what he lacks, of the priapic which has been split off from him throughout his life. But unlike Lucius and Encolpius, Aschenbach cannot experience "the bestial degradation of his fall"; for his culture, unlike theirs, regarded all that the dream symbolizes as totally unacceptable. It constitutes all of the dionysian except its beauty, which is personified in Tadzio; and, as we have seen, even to react to that beauty filled Aschenbach with uncontrollable shame.

But Tadzio nevertheless symbolizes all of Dionysus, which includes the priapic. This extreme and overwhelming form of the dionysian explodes into Aschenbach's dream, fighting for assimilation in a psyche whose ego cannot endure it. This is the basis for young Tadzio's fatal power.

Aschenbach's response is pathetic and fatal. As Mann has told us, he personifies "the whole cultural structure of a lifetime," and he cannot abandon his reliance upon this persona. In reality, there are two courses open to him. He can either give up his persona and admit, as Lucius was forced to do, "I am an ass," and then suffer the resulting degradation and humiliation; or he can die. He cannot bear the first, so he guarantees the second.

Aschenbach's behavior after this dream is almost unbearably grotesque. He dyes his hair, and from fussing over his ties, jewelry and cologne, he moves ultimately to applying cosmetics to his aging face.[13] He has misperceived everything. He thinks all he lacks is youth, and that this will bring it to him. Of course he is completely on the wrong track.

His secret obsessional fantasies continue. He follows Tadzio even more compulsively, and he dies, evidently of cholera, while watching the boy on the beach.

Within the contexts of Aschenbach's time, culture and persona, his death is not an unhappy one. He gets as close as possible to that which he lacks, and dies in seemingly happy contemplation of it. To get any closer would involve humiliation, and for Aschenbach hu-

---

[13] Ibid., pp. 69-70.

miliation is an impossibility. Yet when Priapus prunes back inflation, humiliation would appear to be the only recourse. Not to accept it is to die.

It is sufficiently clear that Aschenbach's culture has much in common with our own, and that the ways seemingly open to many men today, when faced with a deflation of the persona with which they have unknowingly identified, are hardly more attractive than those that faced Aschenbach. Some choose spiritual death rather than pursue them. Meanwhile the very many for whom the collapse is not total spend the rest of their lives shoring up the old persona, though the cosmetics become more blatant and more difficult to maintain with every year. It is upon this kind of thing that the desperate excesses of contemporary *machismo* seem based.

And what is the alternative? It is easy to suggest metaphorical palliatives like reunion with *phallos,* assimilation of the dionysian, movement toward *coniunctio,* etc., but the nature of Aschenbach's particular crisis seems to render such platitudes even less helpful than they usually are. Impotence is hard to rationalize, and when the alternative seems morally unacceptable as well as unlikely to succeed (one can hardly argue that Aschenbach should have tried to seduce Tadzio and take him back to Munich) the dilemma is a severe one.

In fact, the classical literary sources suggest that the only alternative is humiliation, and humiliation is hardly more acceptable to men today than it was in 1911 when Mann wrote *Death in Venice.* The admission of physical erotic demands, with all the ecstatic, earthy abandon they bring with them, is apparently more humiliating than Aschenbach can bear.

On the individual level of Aschenbach, rejection of humiliation results in an individual death. It seems to follow that on a collective level, rejection of humiliation can also result in death—but death on a larger scale. It is here that the urgency of the problem of male inflation in our culture becomes apparent, for inflated governments now have the power to choose death rather than humiliation for countless millions of people.

The only conceivable solution would seem to lie in finding some way to facilitate in late-twentieth-century males the kind of transformative humiliation experienced by Encolpius and Lucius. We shall explore this possibility in part two, through the dreams and analyses of modern men, but first let us briefly examine the physical symptoms of extreme priapic inflation.

The phallus as philosophical tree in alchemy.
(14th cent.; Biblioteca Mediceo-Laurenziana, Florence)

4

Physical Priapism

Priapism (pri´a-pizm) [L. *priapus* (q.v.), penis]. Persistent erection of the penis, especially when due to disease or excessive quantities of androgens, and not to sexual desire.

—*Stedman's Medical Dictionary,* 1976.

That psyche and soma are ultimately indivisible is becoming more and more apparent as we come to understand the physical manifestations of psychological conditions, and vice versa. Therefore, we would be remiss not to look at the medical literature describing the condition named after our god. As we shall see, the physical pathology provides a very concrete amplification of our mythic material.

To begin with, physical priapism is rare. One author of a medical manual states that he has seen fewer than ten "persistent" cases in his career as a urologist.[1] It appears that true priapism—that is, prolonged penile erection unaccompanied by sexual desire, often accompanied by pain and involving engorgement only of the corpora cavernosa—is not infrequently associated with leukemia and with sickle cell disease.

Also mentioned in the literature as causes are infections (especially of the prostate), disease of the central nervous system, trauma and tumors,[2] and thrombosis of the veins of the corpora cavernosa, often supposedly due to sexual excess.[3] This latter situation and the number of cases lacking an obvious definite cause comprise the category of "idiopathic priapism," which is the form of concern to us here. It

---

[1] Alec W. Badenoch, *Manual of Urology,* p. 549.
[2] J.T. Grayhack, "Early Shunting Procedures in the Treatment of Priapism," p. 382.
[3] Fletcher H. Colby, *Essential Urology,* pp. 515-516.

results in impotence if not treated promptly, but prompt treatment is no guarantee of restoration of potency once priapism has occurred.

Colby gives a description of priapism which is both thorough and compact::

> True priapism is a pathological condition of prolonged erection unaccompanied by sexual desire. It may occur at any age.
>
> **Etiology:** The causes of priapism are varied and often obscure. Hinman divided priapism into two groups: 1. those nervous in origin, and 2. those due to mechanical causes.
>
> *Priapism due to nerve origin.* Stimuli may be peripheral or come from the spinal cord or brain. Many of the reported cases of priapism were associated with diseases of the spinal cord such as injury, degenerative lesions, or neoplasms pressing on the cord. Others were due to cerebral injuries or cerebellar tumors.
>
> *Priapism due to mechanical causes.* Thrombosis of the veins of the corpora cavernosa is the commonest mechanical cause of priapism. Many cases are due to thrombosis following sexual excesses. Others are due to infection, local or generalized. Some are caused by neoplasms of the penis. About twenty-five per cent of cases of priapism have occurred in patients with leukemia or similar disorders. Several cases of priapism recently have been reported in colored patients who had sickle cell anemia.
>
> **Symptoms:** In true priapism there usually is erection only of the corpora cavernosa. The onset is sudden, usually with pain. Urination may be difficult or impossible. Ejaculation is possible but the condition persists unchanged.
>
> **Diagnosis:** Blood examinations should be performed on all cases of priapism to determine if leukemia or sickle cell anemia is present. A through search for enlarged lymph nodes should be made. Priapism persisting for over a week usually is mechanical in origin.
>
> **Treatment:** Some cases of priapism get well spontaneously. Those due to thrombosis often are relieved by aspiration, with a large bore needle, of thick dark blood from the cavernous spaces. Incision and drainage of the corpora cavernosa may be required. It has been suggested that priapism due to nerve lesions be relieved by blocking or sectioning the pudic nerves in the perineum. When priapism complicates sickle cell anemia, multiple small blood transfu-

sions are given. When there is thrombosis of the veins of the corpora cavernosa, dicumarol in daily doses of 100 to 300 mg. is advised to get the prothrombin level to about twenty-five per cent of normal. The prothrombin level must be carefully watched.

Prognosis: Impotence may follow priapism.[4]

While a good deal of the literature on priapism is given over to descriptions of surgical treatments, such treatments commonly fail to restore full erectile functioning.[5] One hears echoes of our myth already: Priapus prunes but does not restore inflation.

"The first 72 hours of idiopathic priapism are critical in achieving a successful outcome," writes C.C. Winter, "since irreversible fibrosis usually occurs to some degree after that period of unrelieved turgidity."[6] This fibrosis provides the most fascinating concretization of the myth; for, in the words of Winter, "In the late stages of priapism, fibrosis of the corpora cavernosa occurs, so that the penis develops a woody condition and may remain moderately enlarged."[7] That is to say, the penis becomes a usually impotent, "woody" column, just like the altar at which Priapus's sacrifices were made in classical times. At this point, surgery provides no cure:

> Loss of potency and failure to achieve detumescence are a consequence of persistent priapism or resultant fibrosis of the cavernous bodies and not a complication of the shunting procedure.[8]

Of course one is instantly led to wonder: is there evidence of an inflationary splitting off of any kind that precedes this distressing condition? For if the condition itself so resembles a concretization of Priapus's mythic revenge, and forces its unfortunate victim into an impotent daily awareness of his altar, we would wish to find out how the victim previously ignored his duty to sacrifice to the vengeful god.

---

[4] Ibid., pp. 315-316.

[5] Badenoch, *Manual of Urology,* p. 549.

[6] *The Nonoperative Management of Priapism,* p. 374.

[7] Ibid.

[8] Grayhack, "Early Shunting Procedures," p. 384.

Obviously, such a question is not easy to answer. Yet I think we can find two clues. One is in Colby's attribution, quoted above, of a number of cases of priapism to thrombosis brought on by sexual excess. Sexual excess is by itself an inflation, in that it inflates the phallus by attempting to concentrate all of *phallos* in its corporeality. It would be possible, then, to see this as a metaphor for the inflation that accompanies any kind of excess; and excesses of power, strength, wealth, stamina, money, alcoholic capacity and so on are certainly part of the late-twentieth-century masculine inflation we are here addressing.

Conscious sacrifice of one's excesses will have an obviously deflating effect, as those who left parts of their crops at the foot of Priapus's column clearly knew. At least in the realm of sexual excess, then, the god apparently has a physiological way of getting his sacrificial due if one becomes so inflated as to deny him.

The other clue is to be found in Rafael López-Pedraza's *Hermes and His Children*, which has a chapter on Priapus. López-Pedraza chooses to focus on the generality of Priapus's "freakishness" rather than on the specific image of the outsized genitals. This turns his discussion away from the primary significance of the genitals themselves, and renders much of it peripheral to our purpose here. However, in the course of his research he interviewed some patients who had had surgery for priapism, and he has this to say about them:

> I was able to talk with some post-surgical patients of Priapism. One has the same picture of those extremes of potency and irreparable weakness. To one's amazement, they have no sexual fantasies and, if one hints at sexual fantasies, their immediate reaction is that they have an absolutely "normal" sexuality. They repeat the word "normal" in a tremendously convincing way. During conversations with these patients, there was little or nothing I could gather to put me on the track of any movement towards what we call a psychical sexuality, or memories of sexual images. I had no impression of a life's tragedy, or drama, or even of a disturbed sexuality, or anything like that, only that constant repetition of the word "normal." "I am perfectly normal," "I have always had a very normal sexuality," etc.
>
> But there was something more, something I would like to add to the language of the children of Priapus, the rhetoric of Priapus. One

patient told me about his sexuality only in terms of times and time. It was always normal. It could be two or three times or four times a week. It lasted sometimes for two hours, or two hours and a half; sometimes four hours, or five hours, sometimes six hours, or six hours and a half. I would like to add his language to the rhetoric of Priapus we are tracking down.[9]

This patient's language is a good example of what López-Pedraza calls "the rhetoric of Priapus." He stresses its repetitiveness, its stupidity and its banality. To me, there is something more central to it, which harks back to the priapic physiopathology itself: its utter concreteness. There is no sense of metaphor, no receptivity to symbol, no ability to fantasize, not even an openness to analogy or simile. Everything is concrete, and is exactly what it is. *Phallos* is phallus is intercourse is flesh-and-blood orgasm—exclusively. The denial of the symbolic, and therefore of the psychological, is total.

This seems to me to echo Petronius, Apuleius and Thomas Mann. Each of their heroes concretizes his phallic quest and therefore renders it hopeless. Aschenbach so fears the concrete quest that he cannot even embark upon it; Encolpius appears to concretize his phallos even when it is restored to him, thus seeming to endanger it all over again; and only Lucius, after a long struggle, is able to accept himself as what he is—an ass—without the concrete trappings of male power and position. The impossible demand is that Priapus restore the inflated state he has pruned, to its original concrete form. This is the same as the demand for a total reversal of the fibrosis that results from priapism.

But it cannot happen. The cure comes from another god or goddess, when it comes at all; and, in the case of Lucius, the only "priapic" hero whose further evolution we know about, it requires a total change in the expression of *phallos*. It requires a move toward the metaphoric, the religious, the psychological and the feminine. It is just such a receptivity to metaphor that López-Pedraza's interviewees evidently lack.

---

[9] *Hermes and His Children*, p. 130.

We can speculate that this lack of ability to experience *phallos* psychologically, that is symbolically, might be what caused the excessive concretization in the first place. Then the sacrifice Priapus demands becomes the sacrifice of material excess and the inflated persona that accompanies identification with it. Sacrifice of persona leads to humiliation, which does not remit unless one finds one's way to psychological, metaphoric fulfillment of that which one had been trying to satisfy concretely.

We shall now look to dreams and ways in which the psyche itself may provide the means to this sacrifice.

Priapic Mercury.
(wall painting, possibly from Pompeii, reign of Nero;
National Museum, Naples).

Part Two
The Phallic Quest

5
Stages of the Phallic Quest

What we have so far is a mythologem which has elaborated itself through mythical, literary, psychological and physical metaphors. If we combine and summarize this material, the story emerges in seven stages which are discernible in all of its forms. Furthermore, dreams and life-situations of men in whom this priapic archetype has been activated reflect the same stages, somewhat as indicators of what part of the phallic journey the unconscious is meditating upon at the time of the dream.

The seven stages group themselves in three larger phases of the myth, providing a kind of ternary structure with an exposition, development and resolution. These are outlined below. Each of the following chapters will be devoted to one of these phases.

Phase	Stage
I. Exposition	1. Splitting off
	2. Inflation
II. Development	3. Pruning
	4. Quest
	5. Abandonment of the quest
III. Resolution	6. Divine intervention
	7. Transformation

It must be understood that though they are sequential, these stages operate in psycho-mythical time. Therefore, as in any mythic sequence of events, all of its parts are happening always, and movement occurs as the individual or cultural psyche moves within the perpetual, transpersonal myth.

This is to say that we cannot expect orderly progress in any given case. Rather, stages are repeated and returned to until they are adequately assimilated by the ego. Furthermore, not all who enter the journey reach the end. For example, Aschenbach's story stops at stage 5, and Encolpius, at least in the surviving fragments of the *Satyricon,* reaches stage 6. Of the classical heroes we have discussed, only Lucius reaches the final transformation.

6

Phase I: Exposition

Splitting Off

Priapus, as we have noted, is a fragment. Like the lost phallus of Osiris, he is a part of a divine image which underwent an evolution that excluded him as the image of Dionysus evolved from the bearded man to the beautiful adolescent.

Psychologically, then, we can say that whenever the masculinity which appeals to Aphrodite—that is to say, which is sexually charged in an individual psyche or culture—moves toward the adolescent, the adult *phallos* which cannot be contained in the adolescent image takes on an autonomous identity. Priapus is born.

In the Greek and Roman worlds in which Priapus was worshipped, this adolescent male image appears to have been a consciously cultivated, culture-wide esthetic ideal. This is not precisely the case in twentieth-century Western culture. It is true that with us the adolescent male appears as a physical ideal in some individual psyches, some family systems (especially when the mother-son relationship becomes sexualized) and in some largely homosexual subcultures. However, on the contemporary culture-wide level, what is "worshipped" appears to be an adolescent male psyche, more than the adolescent male body of Greece and Rome. That is to say, our rites of passage into manhood are debased and ineffective.

"It has often been said that one of the characteristics of the modern world is the disappearance of any meaningful rites of initiation," writes Mircea Eliade.[1] Joseph Henderson's *Thresholds of Initiation* documents the psyche's efforts to compensate for this phenomenon, while Thorkil Vanggaard has discussed the effects of phallic initia-

---

[1] *Rites and Symbols of Initiation,* p. ix.

77

tion, and the lack of it, upon masculine development in Western culture.[2]

For example, the Jewish bar mitzvah is probably the most extensively practiced such rite remaining in America today; but afterward the young male goes home to his family, to live exactly as he did before. Nowhere is there a formal, irreversible movement from mother-dependency to adult phallic independence. Thus generation after generation of males is left psychologically adolescent for extended periods, if not for entire lifetimes, while *phallos* necessarily becomes an independent complex, perpetually holding men in helpless bondage to all kinds of power exercises and sports.

By itself, the splitting off of *phallos* does not appear to inflict the kind of pain on a man that drives him to psychotherapy. I suspect that classical culture's adolescent-dionysian esthetic survived as long as it did for this reason. But masculinity split from *phallos* is peculiarly subject to inflation, especially as now there is no phallus, metaphorically speaking, to be legitimately inflated. Inflation tends to happen then to whatever is available, which, after the split, is ego.

Classical cultures knew this, and seem to have warded it off by sacrificing a portion of men's labor to Priapus, thus preventing an inflated sense of one's material or psychological wealth. But our culture has no such built-in sacrificial procedure, leaving men in whom *phallos* is split off vulnerable to the inflation (stage 2) that Priapus prunes (stage 3). It is the pain of the pruning, or deflation, that brings a number of them into therapy.[3]

Thus, our psychological evidence will come largely from men actually dealing with the middle or "development" phase of the myth. (It might almost as well be called a phase of analysis.)

One such man, whom I shall call Robert, experienced the following vision in the course of an active imagination; it vividly describes

---

[2] *Phallos: A Symbol and Its History in the Male World.*

[3] This is dramatically illustrated in Daryl Sharp, *The Survival Papers: Anatomy of a Midlife Crisis.*

the splitting off of *phallos* which results from a mother's overidealization of her prepubertal son.

> I saw a witch, a warty, white-haired old crone with a black robe and a pointed hat. She had a big caldron which she stirred with a broom of twigs, as it boiled over a fire in a clearing surrounded by woods. I approached her and saw myself as a boy, perhaps ten or eleven years old. As soon as I got near her, she pulled the broom out of the caldron and used it like a paintbrush to paint the boy with liquid from head to foot. She did this violently, hitting him with the broom and splashing the liquid around. The boy turned into a girl. He was especially aware of the changed shape of the crotch of his underpants, for he no longer had a penis. Then I became aware of the girl's development over the next years. She seemed to stay in the woods, and grew into a beautiful, sexy, mysterious young woman with long black hair.

Robert had actually spent his adolescence as a kind of brooding, dark-haired Tadzio, lost in the woods of an intimate, overheated relationship with his mother and the hostile jealousy of his narcissistic father. Terrified of what he experienced as his shamefully effeminate nature, he turned to so-called manly activities wholly inconsistent with his creative temperament. He was not good at them, naturally, and developed a sense of incompetence which continually undermined him professionally and led to his starting analysis.

The theme of transsexualism caused by a castrating witch also occurs in Stephen's material; but evidently for him the bewitchment occurred at an earlier age. At the beginning of his analysis, Stephen said he had had a number of witch dreams at ages three, four and five, and cited the following as typical:

> I'm in my mother's bedroom, watching her undress. She becomes a witch. I run to my mother (another) outside, but she too turns into a witch.

Stephen had the following dream after telling this; it relates the witch to his psychologically castrated state:

> I'm worried about finishing my examinations. This is more like grade-school classes. Then, I'm in a room, I'm a girl with long blonde hair and a party dress on. This tall, hawk-faced, black-haired

woman in a tight Victorian dress with a high collar is at the other end of the room. She's about to discipline me for being a witch and not behaving, but she tells me a secret, that she too was a witch when she was young; and she lets me know that if I behave enough she'll let me do whatever I want.

Judging by prepubertal memories and dreams brought to analysis by other men, it is possible that the splitting off of phallic potential is experienced by boys as irrational fears of really being girls. Though beyond the scope of this book, it would be fascinating to explore the geneses of transsexualism and transvestism within the framework of the Priapus myth.

Here is another transsexual dream, this one from David, whose case will be discussed more extensively in the next chapter:

I'm with a girl from first grade. She refers to me as a girl, and asks what's wrong with me.

Inflation

It would appear that the postpubertal male who has been separated from the possibility of psychological connection with *phallos* is peculiarly subject to inflation, which occurs as a defense against the disturbing experiencing of himself as feminine.

Classical culture regarded inflation as dangerous, for it made one vulnerable to Priapus's drastic reductions; therefore sacrifices were made to prevent it. Our culture does no such thing. Since inflation by itself is anything but painful, men do not come into therapy while able to maintain it. Rather, they seem to break down when the maintenance of a previous inflated state has become impossible for one reason or another: a failed relationship, a lost job, decline of the physical attributes of youth, or anything else upon which they had become overdependent for their sense of importance or male identity in the world.

For instance, Encolpius's inflation appears to have been in his sense of himself as both limitlessly sexual and above the religious and legal strictures of his world. Lucius's was that he could dominate magic. Aschenbach's inflation was in his total identification with his status as an important author.

In our time, men in analysis often return again and again to inflated states, unable to sacrifice the persona-attributes which blow them up beyond their realities. The following dreams of inflation contain a selection of the many metaphors in which the psyche describes this state. No doubt any analyst could add many others.

This dream is from Robert, in whose family a castrated/inflated masculinity seems to have been the norm for some generations:

> I take the dog to my maternal grandparents' house. We go along an old footpath, the dog running along the ground while I float in the air behind him, connected to him by a long leash. Then I repeat the trip, this time bringing my father along. Again the dog runs ahead, and either my father walks while I float or I walk while he does. The next day we do it again, with my brother walking along with my father while I float behind the dog.

Robert was well into his analysis at the time of this dream, which seems to reflect an increasing groundedness in his masculinity as he repeats the path—naturally, with ego staying inflated longest. This kind of repetition appears inevitable, for the pain of deflation of the false ego-stance and the resultant acceptance and assimilation of one's actual castrated, impotent split-off state can be very difficult to face all at once.

Stephen brought the following dream early in his analysis. Interestingly, he reported having reread *Death in Venice* the day before. (At that time I had not yet begun investigating the myths of inflation, so we did not talk of Mann's story in that context. Stephen's psyche seemed to have gotten the point, nevertheless.) The dream's ending suggests how he experienced himself when his inflations burst. No wonder he returned to them so obstinately!

> I'm with my family. Then I'm in the theater at college. An act is onstage, and I realize I am the third act. They announce "Batman is on," and I swoop down in costume and make an exaggerated bow, though the people are already applauding. Then I swoop back again, exuberantly. A man comes on stage and says, "I'm God." I go back and make derisive jokes about the college. I find I can't stop without

winding down; and when I finally do, it's all disappeared and I'm all alone.

The following dreams of Arnold's, all from one night, will serve to illustrate some other metaphors for inflation:

I score two key touchdowns in the Superbowl, winning the game. I'm pleased at the publicity, that I've done well and my name is on TV. The next day at work, everybody says I got the most valuable player award, but of all the players I'm the worst of them. I say I don't care because I was the most valuable.

I'm playing major league baseball.

I'm supposed to meet the Pope at a business conference. Everyone envisions what it will be like.

It is noticeable that the dreams given here tend not to simply leave the dreamer in an inflated state. Rather compassionately, they imply that some kind of "winding down" is necessary; though even so, the deflated position can be devastating (as in remarks like "I'm all alone," or "Of all the players, I'm the worst").

While we must allow for the fact that these are dreams of men in analysis, and therefore subject to the close psychological scrutiny of another, I think they nevertheless tell us something important about the capacity for self-healing of the inflated psyche. Notwithstanding the message we receive from our culture, psychological inflation is neither normal nor necessary to the maintenance of adult masculinity. The dreams seem to make an effort to lead the dreamers to a more authentic stance, as gently as possible.

7

Phase II: Development

Pruning

In theory, the state of being split from phallos could be maintained indefinitely, if only one could avoid becoming inflated. But inflation is too tempting, as it provides an illusion of masculine identity, the alternative to which is to view oneself as impotent, effeminate or even female.

Sooner or later, however, inflations get punctured, with frequently painful and disastrous results. The puncturing is described in classical myth as Priapus using his knife, and we must see it as the phallic complex's autonomous attempt to call itself to the attention of ego in order to achieve reintegration.

The problem is that the ego resists. Then the complex is compelled to escalate, and the inflation has to be violently attacked, seemingly with no regard at all for ego's well-being. On an individual level this can be disastrous enough; on the collective, cultural level of our time it could be terminally calamitous.

More often than not, inflated men experience deflation as humiliation. Intense or repeated humiliating experiences can bring them to analysis, as they want such experiences to stop. Unfortunately but naturally, they usually want the humiliation to stop by means of restoration of the inflation which they experienced so pleasantly; so the ego state that results from Priapus's pruning is the one we are here calling stage 4, the quest. The pruning initiates the quest for restoration of that which is pruned, and analysis is one of many places men search for restoration.

Therefore, upon entering analysis, many men begin by recounting experiences and dreams of recent deflationary prunings, sometimes with metaphors that precisely mirror aspects of the Priapus myth.

Robert had such a dream, faithful down to the details of the garden and the pear tree, though at the time he was unaware of the mythology of Priapus:

> I drive up a muddy road to a hilltop farm. Each car through makes the road worse, and I have doubts about getting back down again. I have recently planted a pear tree here, and now a couple, friends of mine, go to check for fruit. I start to join them, but feel it is dangerous. They come back with fruit. The man is naked, and I notice he has no penis. He says he has a bell to ring, to warn off people who might be offended by seeing his nakedness.[1]

Robert's associations led to his family, especially to his father's hobby of gardening. "He never seemed to plant anything. He was always pruning, mowing, cutting back, killing the weeds and poisoning the bugs. I think he did the same thing to me," he said. In fact, Robert had a somewhat inflated view of his adolescent potential, for he was inclined to view himself as a ruined child prodigy; but as a description of how it feels to encounter Priapus's knife, his association is eloquent.

Stephen had a similar dream in which the pruning and sense of castration are expressed more metaphorically but in which the sense of humiliation is vivid. He had an inflated view of his place among his business associates, and the deflating humiliations and strained personal relationships he therefore experienced were very painful to him. They eventually undermined his position to the point that he had to leave that job.

> I'm undressing at the end of a workday. My boss and an associate of his pass by. I'm embarrassed to be found naked, and pretend I'm dressing, but don't put on my underwear. Even so, they leave without me.

Also of note is the following dream of Arnold's, at a time of dealing with an inflation described in the dream as a "big thing." It con-

---

[1] It is worth noting that dreams of disrobing and nakedness in public, suggesting a disidentification from the persona, may occur during the process of deflation.

tains imagery of pruning, with suggestions that the inflation is due to a mother attachment:

> A gang of pre-teenage boys does some complicated thing that is involved with me, possibly against me. Then one of them does some big thing, so he is entitled to take a small knife and make cuts on the bridges of two other boys' noses. As he does this—by putting the blade against the nose and hitting it with his hand—he says, ritually, "Mom got you a cut on the nose, in broad daylight."

Suggestions of a social humiliation ("a cut . . . in broad daylight") and of phallic displacement to the nose also emerged in Arnold's associations. We did not explore why the knife was small, though it could have to do both with a kind of anti-inflationary quality connected with the "cut" and with the reality that pruning knives are usually not large.

The Quest

It is difficult to isolate the pruning stage from the resulting quest for the restoration of the inflated state, for the quest starts immediately, and it is in its course that most men come to analysis.

Quite often, their quest has been long, for it is almost always a quest for restoration of the inflation, rather than for a positive sense of *phallos* that would permit them to live without it. To turn their quest in a more fruitful direction becomes the work of the analysis, and so it requires the abandonment of desire for the inflated state and conscious grieving over its loss.

Lucius's quest, of course, is for restoration of his human state, which implies restoration of his inflated view of himself as a kind of anthropologist of magic. Aschenbach's is less clearly delineated, and the fact that he cannot clearly face even the image of its goal—the seduction of Tadzio—is probably responsible for the impossible bind he escapes only through death. Encolpius's quest most resembles a form in which we frequently meet it in analytic work today, which is the active quest for sex.

David will provide an example. He complained of frequent compulsive sexual encounters with anonymous men he met in bars, baths, parks and so on.[2] They were never very satisfactory, and after them he became extremely depressed and upset with himself; yet he was unable to change or understand his behavior.

His mother hated the memory of his deceased father, whom David had never known and whom he physically resembled. Therefore the mother did all she could to undermine anything in David, including his masculinity, that reminded her of his father. She became a "castrating mother." It was as if, in her mind, men died and caused her problems, so she set out to prevent her son from becoming one. As a child David spent hours fantasizing that his father would magically return, "come walking down the hill and make me happy."

Early in analysis David recounted the following dream, which he remembered from his preschool years:

> It's dark outside, somebody comes down the hill to our house. It's erotic, a huge, nude, hairy man. There's something very red about the head of his penis. I remember security, warmth and excitement in touching his legs or something.

David regarded this dream as an early statement of his homosexual orientation, but I think there is more in it than that. The image of the man is priapic. If intimate contact with Priapus provides security, warmth and excitement (all of which had been absent from David's childhood), then the dream explicitly presents the split from *phallos* that needs to be healed if David is to experience these qualities in his adult life. Men who were phallic in the sense of the dream were those David sought out, concretizing the image of the complex he needed to contact within.

A second dream, shortly before his first analytic hour, gives an image of the fragment of Dionysus that remained after the split from *phallos:*

---

2 To put David's behavior in perspective, we should note that this took place before AIDS was known to be associated with this kind of activity.

In a big arena everybody is naked, standing on high bleachers. Nobody has any hair and everybody has a giant green grape between their legs. People are running up the aisles of the bleachers and jumping off the ends.

The lack of *phallos* characterized by the hairless, adolescent Dionysus is here carried to an extreme, for it is replaced by a grape. Perhaps the grape also includes the substitution of alcohol (wine, spirit) for *phallos* that is part of many men's lives—including the world of gay bars, in which David spent a good deal of time. Alcoholism can indeed be a fatally chaotic side of Dionysian ecstasy, here hinted at by the frantic running and jumping in the dream.

A few sessions into analysis, David had the following dream, in which there is an implication that he can begin to look at the symbolic side of his homosexual fixation.

I am told my sister and I have to decorate my mother's house. I start to sabotage the project. I'm afraid of being caught, and run from house to house in the neighborhood. At the end of a house is a door which I open. It leads to the outside, and there in the dark is a naked man, very hot, hairy, a giant penis, definitely gay. I'm immediately attracted. I take a step; and when my foot is right at the middle of the doorway I say, "It's a trap, it's a decoy," and I wake.

Concretization—and perpetuation—of the phallic quest in the form of homosexual promiscuity has been a pervasive phenomenon of our time. It is distressing enough for men who identify themselves as homosexuals, for it endlessly complicates their lives and endangers their deeper relationships. It can be even more painful for men who continue to view themselves as committed to heterosexual relationships. A separation from *phallos* will certainly undermine a man's male-female relationships, for it will leave him powerless to deal with the devouring-mother aspect of any woman with whom he becomes involved. In that event, the temptation to flee to the apparent phallic security of a homosexual encounter can be extreme.

Roger, in his middle twenties, was such a man. He had a long-standing relationship with a young woman who loved him deeply. He was, however, distracted by homosexual fantasies and attrac--

tions; yet when he had an opportunity to act on these urges, he always backed away in panic. He brought the following three dreams after a couple of months of analysis:

> I was introduced to an attractive, rather snotty young woman from my home town. She asked if I had a boy friend, as if I were gay. I said no, and tried to explain that not everybody from my town was gay, but words started to fail me.

> I'd caught a fish, and set it on the water, hoping it wouldn't float away. It did. I tried to catch it again, but couldn't. It was just out of my grasp. It turned into a pickle.

> I was attracted to a black man, and I found this odd because he was in his thirties.

These dreams are a condensed description of the priapic situation, up to the point we have so far discussed. The attraction to the home-town snotty female suggests an emasculating erotic tie to his mother, which his life's story verified. She was a depressed and unfulfilled woman whom he felt he had to cater to and sustain. The result, the dreams say, is a very tenuous connection with *phallos:* every time he catches it, he tends to put it aside and it floats away. He does not honor it, but devalues it (a caught fish, the awareness of an unconscious content, turns into a pickle), and so he is left in a dilemma (a "pickle") regarding his relationship.

Meanwhile, the dreamer is mysteriously attracted to a dark, unknown, older male figure.

Examples of the phallic quest could be multiplied almost indefinitely. In some men it takes a sexual form, while in others it involves a search for an ideal mentor. Others search for a substitute for a failed or absent father, or for an ideal job, or invention, or elected office, or fortune, or power. The common thing among them all is their exteriorization and concretization of what must at last become an inner quest.

The exteriorized quest cannot make contact with the *phallos* that has been split off within the psyche, so its failure is guaranteed. Therefore, sooner or later, it must be abandoned.

Abandonment of the Quest

If exteriorization, or concretization, of the priapic quest is what guarantees its failure, then we can understand the peculiar relevance of the concretization in the medical syndrome of priapism which we observed in chapter four.

Yet Priapus seems to require concretization of his imagery if we are to experience him at all. In this fact seems to be the explanation of his most difficult characteristic: he cannot restore that which he prunes. He prunes an inflated viewpoint, and inflation is only deflated by a confrontation with objective reality—"in broad daylight," as Arnold's dream (above, p. 85) puts it. The result is humiliation, which is another "real world" phenomenon in that it is not experienced intrapsychically.

True, painful humiliation seems to require at least two participants, for it involves fear of another's rejection as well as powerlessness to prevent it. Priapus prunes, deflates, humiliates and departs from the scene. At this point one has two alternatives: either one starts another, equally doomed cycle of inflation or one abandons the quest altogether, submitting to humiliation as the price of liberation.

Lucius, for instance, abandons his image of himself as a connoisseur of magic. Aschenbach abandons his delusions of youthful potential, and with them, his life. We do not know for sure what Encolpius abandons, for the end of the surviving text is not complete enough to tell.

Of the men whose dreams are recounted here, two of them had to abandon established professions in which they and their families had become heavily invested; one abandoned a public religious commitment he had believed to be a vocation; one abandoned a marriage he deeply wanted to succeed; and two abandoned "sexual identities" which they had proclaimed with all the public fanfare that goes with the politicized sexuality characteristic of our time.

All found these acts of sacrifice humiliating, for they required renunciation of inflated personae in which the men had invested significant parts of their lives, and from which they had expected gratification in the form of confirmation from the people around them. Giving up this expectation meant a terrifying confrontation with the possibility—and often the reality—of rejection by people who were very important to them.

Furthermore, there is no guarantee that the sacrifices they have so far made are enough; further inflations, prunings and humiliations may lie in store for any or all of them.[3]

In terms of the myth, this amounts to abandonment of the idea that Priapus is going to restore what he has taken away. It is experienced as an acceptance of one's impotence, one's castration, as a permanent-seeming state, or as acceptance of a man's childhood fear that he is, after all, shamefully effeminate, separated forever from the world of men—a girl. Experienced without metaphor, in the concretism of what López-Pedraza calls "the "rhetoric of Priapus," it must result in permanent impotence, as was the case with the surgical patients cited in chapter four.

Lucius's story seems to provide the most eloquent statement of the loss and recovery of *phallos* that we have, and as we investigate the latter phases of this process we shall draw upon it more and more. What Lucius seems to abandon could easily be called a bewitchment—that is, a fatally inflated fascination with witches and their practices—which of course parallels the frequently encountered mother-bewitchment theme we mentioned above in connection with the splitting off of *phallos* in contemporary men.

In fact, Lucius abandons more than an inflated fascination. He has to abandon all desire to live as he did before his transformation, even to abandoning desire to live at all. As von Franz puts it,

He has reached the deepest place . . . the bottom of misery. He has gone through personal tragedy in his bitter experiences and now to the sea, the border of the collective unconscious. For the first time,

---

[3] See Eugene Monick, *Phallos: Sacred Image of the Masculine,* particularly pp. 15 and 45, for a description of this process in more detail, and examples of the "castration anxiety" that a shaky relationship to *phallos* commonly entails.

Lucius's adventures as an ass.
(from Apuleius, *Les Metamorphoses ou l'Asne dor*, 1648)

Lucius rejects involvement with people and tries to be himself with his own misery and loneliness, and in this state of exhaustion falls asleep.[4]

And again,

For the first time, he does not even ask to go on living. He is weary of life, not even caring whether she [Isis, the moon goddess, to whom, as *Regina coeli,* he addresses a prayer] grants him a continuation of life or releases him through death. The only thing he asks is that she will give him back to himself. Such is the essence of Tao in which the ego can partake when confronted with fate. Not to want this or that, to give up the ego-will which would like this, that, and the other, not to want to live or die or no longer to suffer. He has been worn down to realize that nothing matters except that he might again be himself.[5]

Aschenbach makes a similar abandonment, also by the sea; for he becomes utterly what he is, the "watcher" of Tadzio, with no inflated pretense of anything else and without expectation of any consequences. The old Aschenbach, the respected writer, will never be again; he receives a dream and is transformed in the only way open to him, through death. For both him and Lucius, the quest for restoration of that which they were before is ended.

As Stephen neared the point of abandoning an inflated and destructive professional commitment, he had the following dream (note that the names Jim and Willie closely resemble my own):

I'm standing alone at a bar. A movie star, Jim, walks by me and then turns back and puts his arm around me from the back.

Then I'm in India. An evil and crazed man has been knifing people and drives by me on the road. Others and I take out after him. Willie and someone else corner him. Willie's fighting him and about to get seriously cut when I arrive—Willie's too young for this, he's not responsible. I take over with a feeling of fatalism with a long, long ceremonial sword, and while the madman is lying down, let it fall once, on his crotch, and then a final blow on his heart, which

---

[4] *A Psychological Interpretation of the Golden Ass of Apuleius,* p. 137.
[5] Ibid, p. 139.

kills him. I then walk away, still with a sense of sad fate, facing the sun.

Stephen was able to identify the madman as his own professional grandiosity. For a long time, he had regarded himself as more important to his firm than his employers did, and so he constantly exceeded his authority in a touchy, defensive way which managed to offend anyone who became closely involved with him. The dream message regarding the profound necessity for him to take full responsibility for killing this off was unmistakable. His analyst could not do it.

Within six weeks of this dream Stephen initiated far-reaching and, to himself and his family, humiliating changes in his professional identity.

Marble pillar with head of Hermes.
(6th cent. B.C.; National Museum, Athens)

8
Phase III: Resolution

Divine Intervention

Discussion of the third phase of the quest takes us into relatively rarefied territory. Of our original three literary guides, Encolpius and Aschenbach are left behind, and only Lucius remains to illustrate in detail the way in which *phallos* can—but need not—return, through the intervention of a divinity other than Priapus.

It seems similar in analysis. The abandonment of the phallic quest can in itself be a fulfillment of the analytic process, leaving one simply to live as he really is, uninflated and in the present of his daily rounds. Freud's often-quoted verdict comes to mind, that the goal of analysis is the ability "to work and to love."

Thus, consideration of this third phase can carry us beyond a discussion of analysis. For some, renewed—or perhaps the first—contact with *phallos* and subsequent transformations in their way of life will come in the context of analysis; but for many others, these things may come to fruition only after the formal analytic process has ended. The point to be investigated here, however, is the psychological situation when energy is no longer devoted to a quest for renewed inflations.

While we lack much that Petronius said on this subject, from him we know that *phallos* does return, and that it is returned not by the god who took it, but by Hermes.[1]

Hermes' slippery, duplicitous characteristics make him a likely carrier of that which one experiences as having been mysteriously stolen. Furthermore, he is one of the Olympians, in every way a more universal god than Priapus. This suggests that when the

---

[1] The *Satyricon,* p. 163.

Satyr and herm, detail of a marble sarcophagus.
(2nd cent. A.D., from the Farnese Museum; National Museum, Naples)

formerly separate, autonomous phallic complex is autonomous no longer, Priapus as a separate entity disappears from the scene. He is not necessary once an authentic connection with *phallos* is established.

We do not know what this meant for Encolpius's life. But if we consider the priapic mythology as a whole, it would seem reasonable to suggest that the restoration of *phallos* requires that it be experienced in a less concrete manner than in the original "rhetoric of Priapus." In other words, *phallos* moves from the realm of exterior reality to the realm of psychological metaphor.

This seems to be the meaning of what happens when Isis reassembles Osiris's dismembered body; for though she never finds his penis, through the intervention of a divine grace from beyond even the realm of these immense deities, she conceives a child by him. The child, Horus, comes to replace Osiris, which suggests that a new individuality, undivided, is the goal of this process.

Apuleius gives us the last two phases of the quest in detail. In Lucius's case, his abandonment of all inflation—indeed, of all desire for ego, and even for life—results in the intervention of Isis herself. In exchange for a promise to change his life entirely and become initiated into her mysteries, Isis arranges for Lucius's human form to be restored.

The initiation is difficult. It is described in some detail, though the finale is withheld as a secret not to be revealed outside the cult. After a strenuous period of living in the temple, observing dietary restrictions and chastity, and reporting his dreams to the priests, a climax is reached:

> I will record as much as I may lawfully record for the uninitiated [says Lucius], but only on condition that you believe it. *I approached the very gates of death and set one foot on Proserpine's threshold, yet was permitted to return, rapt through the elements. At midnight I saw the sun shining as if it were noon; I entered the presence of the gods of the underworld and the gods of the upperworld, stood near and worshipped them.*

Isis with Horus.
(2040-1700 B.C., copper sculpture, from Egypt;
Staatliche Museen, Berlin)

Well, now you have heard what happened, but I fear you are none the wiser.

The solemn rites ended at dawn and I emerged from the sanctuary.
. . .

The curtains were pulled aside and I was suddenly exposed to the gaze of the crowd, as when a statue is unveiled, dressed like the sun. That day was the happiest of my initiation, and I celebrated it as my birthday with a cheerful banquet at which all my friends were present. Further rites and ceremonies were performed on the third day, including a sacred breakfast, and these ended the proceedings. However, I remained for some days longer in the temple, enjoying the ineffable pleasure of contemplating the Goddess's statue, because I was bound to her by a debt of gratitude so large that I could never repay it.[2]

Lucius's initiation requires a total commitment, so he is effectively forced to experience his masculine wholeness (his human form) in religious metaphor, not through concrete worldly events such as literal transformation into an animal and the inflating magical powers he had formerly sought.

What does this mean for men in our time? If Priapus is integrated and disappears, we must assume that the anima fascination for the adolescent masculinity that gave him birth is also ended. The tentative, mother-dependent, collectively-oriented adolescent stance toward the world, which underlies the inflations, will be replaced by a sense of oneself as a man who is capable of potentiating his own individual destiny. Inflation would seem to become a psychological improbability, for it is no longer necessary to erect defenses against the sense of being impotent and effeminate that dogs the man without authentic phallic resources.

When a man seeks to experience *phallos* concretely, in the world, we can expect that he will see *phallos* everywhere he looks. For example, the man whose phallic quest takes the form of a search for sex with other males seems to seek and find partners wherever he goes. Or again, the man whose phallic quest takes the form of a search for

---

[2] Apuleius, *The Golden Ass,* pp. 279-281 (italics in the original).

power or dominance will find individuals or situations or nations (if he is politically ambitious) that seem to require him to dominate them. The world takes on a form congruent with the projected phallic imagery.

Now when the man no longer feeds his inflation with a continuing quest, but experiences *phallos* within and unprojected, *phallos* loses the concreteness of the objective world. Here, two things happen: *phallos* takes its proper place as part of psyche, not of the material world, and the material world is freed of the constraints of the man's projection, so it can be seen for what it is.

Transformation

Anyone who for the first time experiences his surroundings without projection truly experiences a transformation, which extends literally beyond himself. He sees the world anew, more nearly as it really is. He experiences *phallos* as libido—psychic energy—with which to engage this world.

Something of this sort seems finally to happen to Lucius, as he takes up further religious initiations into the mysteries of Osiris and—very importantly—as he moves into a totally new profession and station in life, becoming a successful lawyer in Rome.

In and after analysis, the transformation seems usually not to come all at once, and so it is seldom as dramatic as Lucius's. Rather, *phallos* is returned bit by bit, in different areas of one's life. One might say it is brought back by several different gods, and that the divine intervention is experienced repeatedly.

One example of such a return has already been cited as Stephen's sword dream (above, p. 92). We might hypothesize that the *phallos* he wields was brought by Athena, or perhaps by Ares, but there is not sufficient material in our sources to draw firm conclusions.

Another man, Patrick, had a dream that indicates an intervention by a power beyond himself—call it a god, or an inner guiding center, the Self—in the form of a driverless car:

I was walking home. A young black woman offered me a ride in a black limousine. When I got in I was startled to find that the car had no driver. I asked the girl about this, and she said it was programmed to get us to the destination. Just as we arrived it swerved to the left, off the road into what had once been a wooded lot, but was now paved over with asphalt. "Oh, no," I said, "Don't tell me they've paved over the only bit of green left around here."

Discussion revealed that the dream referred to quite specific aspects of Patrick's life. For years he had worked in increasingly idealistic ways in inner city areas. He had become inflated about the self-denial this involved, and his inflation was fed by friends and family who told him how much they admired his involvement in this difficult work. Therefore, when he began to find himself too depressed and apathetic to get up and go to work, he experienced immense guilt and anxiety, which brought him to analysis.

The dream suggested to Patrick that he needed to see his "destination" not in terms of this work, but as something green that grew naturally out of his individuality, his earth; and it led him to make far-reaching changes that transformed his attitude toward himself, what he did and how he did it. Evidently, in the twentieth century, at least one goddess has abandoned her classical chariot for a limousine.

Robert dreamed:

I come home to find a window open and the burglar alarm disconnected. I am quite disturbed that someone has the ability to get in, though nothing has been taken. Then my wife finds a huge, old-fashioned pocket-knife on the floor. It must have been left by the intruder.

At this point in his analysis, Robert was familiar with the mythology of Priapus. He associated the pocket-knife, apparently left behind during a burglary (which activity is reminiscent of Hermes, known for his thieving ways) with Priapus's pruning knife. The necessary connection to the feminine at this point—shown in *The Golden Ass* by the intervention of Isis—seems established here by the fact that it is his wife, not the dreamer himself, who actually picks up the knife.

Robert had this dream at a time when he was beginning to sense his masculine autonomy in his new profession and in his personal life. He said he felt that the knife was now his. The formerly split-off *phallos* was integrated to the point that the knife-wielding god no longer represented an autonomous part of his psyche.

Robert, Stephen and Patrick all saw that their quests could not be renewed; the inflated attitudes that had led to discomfort, humiliation and analysis had had to be abandoned permanently. These were now being replaced by an authentic sense of self, including both individual potentials and very real limitations.

What is a man like when he has reached this point in his psychological journey? The last chapters of Apuleius's *Golden Ass* provide a description that remains meaningful today.

First, Lucius displays a new attitude toward the psyche. From the moment he regains his human shape, he is anxious to do not what he (ego) wants, but what Isis (anima, his inner woman) requires of him. He pays close attention to his dreams. This leads to his initiation into the mysteries of Isis, even though ego is reluctant because of the expense and the stringent vows he is required to take. Then she tells him to go to Rome—again contrary to his desire—and, once there, to be initiated into the mysteries of "the supreme Father of the Gods, the invincible Osiris."[3]

This brings Lucius to another position. It is not sufficient, apparently, to remain in mystical contemplation of the anima and her realm; a man must move on to a relationship with the father archetype, which implies a place in the world, for "the God added that under his divine care [I] would achieve fame in a learned profession."[4] The fees for this initiation took Lucius's last pennies, so he was required to earn money, and he began to make "quite a decent living as a barrister."[5]

---

3 Ibid., p. 284.
4 Ibid., p. 285
5 Ibid., p. 286.

Lucius becomes human again and is initiated into the cult of Isis.
(from Apuleius, *Les Metamorphoses ou l'Asne dor,* 1648)

The need for a third initiation is brought to Lucius's attention "by a kindly god whose name I did not know,"[6] actually Osiris in disguise. A further change in attitude is apparent in the following passage:

> Then once more I fasted, this time voluntarily extending the usual period of abstinence from meat, and paid all the costs out of my own pocket, the scale being dictated by my religious zeal rather than by the requirements of the temple. I had no reason to repent of the trouble and expense, because by the bounty of the gods the fees that I earned in the courts soon compensated me for everything.[7]

In other words, Lucius makes a voluntary sacrifice of material wealth, precisely the anti-inflationary gesture the rites of Priapus would have required of him. Thus, his final initiation seems to have grounded him firmly enough in himself to make him quite resistant to inflationary temptations.

The lines with which Apuleius closes the book seem to confirm this with reference to a masculine phenomenon—fear of losing one's hair—which is especially vulnerable to artificial and inflationary compensations:

> Once more I shaved my head and this time kept it shaved and happily fulfilled the duties of that ancient college. . . . Making no attempt to disguise my baldness by wearing a wig or any other covering, I displayed it without shame on all occasions.[8]

Submission to psyche, attention to dreams, a profession based on an inner vocation, voluntary sacrifice and a religious attitude seem to be the results of Lucius's journey. They protect him at last against the fatal inflationary cycle. Any modern analysis that accomplished as much would have to be called a success.

---

6 Ibid.

7 Ibid., p. 287.

8 Ibid., pp. 287-288.

Conclusions

By way of summary, let us state the elements of the priapic myth in the language of analytical psychology.

We begin with *phallos*—a man's libido, his sense of his ability to potentiate his own destiny, to create himself in accord with his inner image, to treat the demands of the collective as possibilities rather than as obligations. Access to *phallos* is blocked by a sexualized identification with, or fixation on, adolescent masculinity in one or more of its aspects. Being immature, it remains obligated to the demands of the mother and the collective as the price of relatedness to others.

This blockage can be the result of a mother's sexualized transference onto her son; but it can also result from a culture's fixation on the adolescent as a masculine ideal, from a particular relationship's expectations, or from an individual's introjection of the adolescent as a masculine ideal to which he holds himself.

When phallic energy is denied to the conscious awareness of an adult male, it becomes split off. It becomes an autonomous complex, which may be symbolized by the mythical god Priapus. Meanwhile the man's ego, feeling unmasculine or effeminate, compensates with inflationary fantasies and inflated personae in its effort to establish itself in the world. These inflations always seem collectively determined, in that they are efforts to conform to an exterior standard in a way that will compare favorably with that standard, regardless of the actual abilities or personal characteristics of the individual.

Thus Priapus, the split-off complex, becomes a kind of advocate of the interests of the Self, archetype of wholeness and the regulating center of the psyche. But as it has no access to ego's perceptions, it can only strive for integration by acting dramatically *against* ego, calling itself to ego's attention by ruthlessly undermining the inflated positions ego has constructed.

105

Naturally, every success on Priapus's part is experienced by ego as a humiliation which must be escaped as soon as possible; so another inflated position is soon established, and the cycle is repeated until the pain of repeated humiliations drives ego to look more closely at their causes. This kind of examination becomes central in the analysis of these men.

Abandonment of inflation seems impossible without experiencing some degree of humiliation. When a man is able to accept that he is not that which he has intensely striven to be and forced himself to enact, and finally abandons these efforts, Priapus has done his work. The inflationary delusions and ego-dominating personae fall away, leaving the man chastened, but open to influences from the Self which can set him on an authentic course, in harmony with his true individuality. Thus it is that *phallos* is returned by gods other than Priapus.

Of course, to remain receptive to influences from this level of the psyche requires a change in attitude, a "relativization of ego,"[1] which can alter every facet of one's life. Ego and personae no longer determine actions, rather the ego observes what is wanted by the "new gods," the agents of the Self, and tries to implement their desires. For an ego working with this kind of awareness, the monstrous inflation that accompanies ego's attempt to assimilate the Self would become unlikely.

*

Let us also review the major metaphors psyche employs to voice its concerns to the ego threatened by Priapus. (By metaphor, I mean both intrapsychic imagery and psychologically significant patterns or events in an individual's life.) These can be expected to occur in the analyses of a number of men, and their appearance suggests that the

---

[1] In acknowledging the supraordinate authority of the Self, the ego can no longer fancy itself as the center of the psyche. Thus, "the experience of the Self," writes Jung, "is always a defeat for the ego." (*Mysterium Coniunctionis,* CW 14, par. 778)

analyst should pay close attention to the analysand's relationship to *phallos*.

First is the metaphor of bewitchment. It occurs in the histories of Encolpius and Lucius, as well as in the life stories of Robert, Stephen and David. The man's psyche tends to describe a continuing sexually-charged involvement between himself in the form of a bewitched boy and the mother-introject. The bewitchment casts doubt on his gender identity, and can then produce images of transvestism and transsexualism.

Theoretically, transsexualism may have a positive side in an adult, for it could preclude those cycles of inflation and humiliation to which the "bewitched" male is otherwise vulnerable. Anyone who rejects the idea of becoming a man out of hand can hardly succumb to inflated, ego-determined notions of how to be one.

Indeed, we might speculate that the transvestite shamans found among some tribal societies could spring from this kind of early relationship to the mother, and that they gain power and societal roles from their immunity to the enfeebling inflation which competition for male status inflicts upon others.

Thorough treatment of this point would require extensive case material involving transvestism. Nevertheless, speculating about it provided one analysand, Edward, with a starting point in considering his own transvestite practices. This came about as a result of a dream which suggested a connection between transvestism and a powerful phallic complex similar to the one we are discussing.

Edward had said that he enjoyed wearing women's clothing, not because he had any desire to look like a woman, but because in it he felt free from masculine roles he experienced as inauthentic and constraining. He further argued that women often wear men's clothing without anyone thinking it outrageous, and he did not see why the reverse should be true as well. He did not dress blatantly in public situations, but had a circle of intimate friends among whom the practice was accepted. He said the woman he lived with found him "more relational" and easier to get along with when he wore women's clothes.

Edward dreamed:

I am driving my car [a small car he no longer owned] through a park. My brother is with me. I am wearing a skirt and my brother wears pants. I keep trying to arrange my skirt so it will look like shorts, for I am uncertain how my brother will react to it; but he doesn't seem to care. We pass a powerful old convertible, going in the opposite direction. An arrogant-looking man is driving it, and there are three people in the back seat. This man is very rich, he lives in a huge house in the park. My brother says that he once was out driving and had a head-on collision with this man.

The anxiety about the brother's reaction suggests that Edward was not as comfortable with his skirt as he wanted consciously to believe. Nevertheless, there is a clear implication of a dissociated masculine complex that gives him less trouble when he wears a skirt than when he wears trousers. There is also something archaic and depotentiating about this split, for both Edward's small car and the large priapic one are characterized as old.

The dream does not appear to take a stand as to whether the skirt is ultimately more appropriate than the trousers when the complex appears, for neither successfully contacts the riches—the energy—that real integration of the complex would bring. The effect of a thorough working-through of the complex on how Edward dresses is left unknown, but presumably it would involve dealing with a kind of isolated, controlling arrogance, the kind of inflation with which the priapic complex is commonly associated.

Another priapic metaphor is fixation on the phallus and its imagery. This, of course, results from projection of the split-off phallic complex onto the environment. As one might imagine, it can take a great many forms; but I would like to say a bit more about one of its more common courses, which is found in certain kinds of compulsively promiscuous homosexuality. The point to be made is that there is a difference between relatedness between two men, which may or may not involve any kind of overt sexuality, and the kind of compulsive penis-chasing which is a predictable result of denying one's innate *phallos*. Furthermore, compulsive penis-chasing in its most concrete form is not unknown among males who continue to identify themselves as heterosexual.

Therefore, in analyzing men with histories of homosexual fantasies or homosexual experiences, care must be taken to determine what these are about. If it is a question of a split-off phallic complex, corroborating evidence can be found from other aspects of the individual's psychic life. But the analyst needs to be aware that homosexual fantasies and acts which result from a phallic quest seem to have little or nothing to do with the gender of the individual's partner in a long-term relationship.

There is no way to know how many men have made wretched adaptations to a promiscuous and unfulfilling homosexual lifestyle out of the belief that this is what their phallic quests required of them. Stories one hears, however, suggest that there are more than a few. I trust that the cases I mentioned in the preceding chapters make clear that the priapic complex works identically whether the man in question considers himself to be homosexual, heterosexual, bisexual or whatever else.

A related point is implicit in the literary and case material. Among younger males, it seems common for the projection of *phallos* to be made upon older males. David's case provides one example, and Roger's black man dream (above, p. 88) is another. There appears, however, to be a kind of enantiodromia, a reversal of energy, at midlife. Middle-aged men do not as a rule lust compulsively after old ones. Instead, the Priapus image replaces the adolescent Dionysus as the pole with which the subject unconsciously identifies. After this, the man seems to be like a penis looking for a body, rather than the other way around, for he is fascinated with young males who resemble the adolescent Dionysus.

The clearest example here is Gustave von Aschenbach. This point helps to clarify the kind of bafflement Arnold, for instance, felt in recounting his obsession with beautiful young men. He knew he desired contact and intimacy with them, yet sex with them was not especially gratifying to him, and their penises interested him not at all. Metaphorically, he *was* the penis they felt they lacked. Therefore, on

Priapus and Dionysus.
(from William Hamilton, *Collection of Engravings from
Ancient Vases,* 1791)

both sides of the kind of liaison he sought, the psyche's goal was a whole entity composed of body and penis—the undivided Osiris (Horus) or uncastrated Attis—in short, a psychological connection with *phallos*.

We also need to consider the implications of our myth for the phallic quest metaphor itself. The Priapus story suggests that the phallic quest is false. One can search as long as one likes for what one has lost, but one never regains it. One only finds inflation, illusion and humiliation. Priapus prunes but never reconnects. The quest, then, lasts as long as does one's delusion that its object can be found. But the quest's true goal, if it may be called one, is acceptance of failure. It is humiliation. But not a final one; rather it is a humiliation which can lead to transformation.

In analysis, this means that more than intellectual awareness is required of both analyst and analysand. Humiliation occurs in the world, among people. Its acceptance is painful, and men who depend upon inflation for their identity will do almost anything to avoid admitting it into their conscious experience. Yet if they are to get beyond the inflated persona that constantly endangers them and their environment, our material tells us they must experience it deeply.

This brings into question the analyst's ability both to tolerate and to empathize with the humiliated analysand. The analyst must search for whatever unconscious tendency he may harbor to humiliate—which is itself an inflation, based, as many are, on an unconscious sadistic stance. The analyst's own analysis and his experience of his own humiliation are crucial here, for the analyst's task is to sit with his analysand as the latter says, with Lucius, "I am an ass."

The idea that humiliation cannot occur in private leads to the next point, which is the metaphor of concretization that seems to be part of the priapic complex. One can feel deeply ashamed of all kinds of dirty secrets; but until they are revealed to another as enactments in the world, they cannot properly be said to be humiliating. Inflation, to pump one's enactments full of air, is to deconcretize them in an opposite process, and can be seen as the fundamental defense against the humiliating inadequacy of concrete reality. Priapus concretizes, as we saw in chapter four. In dealing with inflation, the analyst must concretize also.

Do we mean, then, that the analyst must—consciously and carefully—humiliate his analysand? In a sense, yes; for the analyst must be the other with whom the analysand experiences humiliation, and must do what is necessary to facilitate this experience.

This is not the place for a discourse on analytic empathy, tact, respect, kindness and love; but it should be evident that these are the kinds of resources the analyst will have to draw upon, sometimes in the face of most unsavory concretizations, if he is going to be elected by the analysand's psyche as the person capable of being there through the humiliation that must occur. Again, an analyst who has worked through what humiliation feels like first-hand is in the best position to succeed in this very delicate process. To avoid it is to prolong the quest, and the analysis, indefinitely.

One more of these metaphors remains; and perhaps it explains the paucity of Priapus's mythology. Priapus is after all a fragment, something that sometimes, but not always, is split off from the masculine whole. He is merely a complex, and as long as he exists he is an obstacle to individuation, for his existence means division. Again we hear echoes of how he prunes but cannot restore. His reintegration is an essential step in the process leading to a masculine indivisibility, that is, to a masculine *individual*. Only as an individual, undivided, can a man continue his journey, meet the feminine as an equal opposite and fulfill his creative destiny.

Priapus is a minor god; but for those for whom he exists at all, his reintegration can become a major project, as we have seen.

*

Lastly, let us consider our material in the larger context of twentieth-century Western culture, in which masculine inflation is ubiquitous. Why should this be, just now?

The answer may lie in our growing awareness of the extent to which the masculine, in the form of patriarchal values, dominates our culture, about which so much has recently been written. As Jung tells us over and over, conscious attitudes are always compensated by their opposite counterparts in the unconscious. In a society as pervasively patriarchal as ours, run by and for men for as long as ours has been, an enormously powerful matriarchal fixation must have been built up in our collective's unconscious structures.

In short, a conscious patriarchy must be unconsciously a matriarchy, which is to say that the patriarchal masculine which runs our society's affairs must have an unconscious, powerfully adolescent tie to the mother archetype. This alone would be enough to start the Priapus cycle on a cultural level, isolating *phallos*, causing male egos to make inflationary substitutes for it, etc.

Here we must be careful to make a distinction between the *unconscious* relationship to the feminine, which is adolescent and matriarchal, and a *conscious* relationship to the feminine, which is phallic, creative and co-equal. This latter is the *coniunctio* out of which new life, individuality, is born. It must be this co-equal relationship that Jung had in mind when he referred to the Faust passage mentioned above in chapter one. We can now see that it is only the uninflated, adult masculine, with full phallic power, that can achieve it.

The goal of reintegration of *phallos* is *coniunctio*, creativity, paternity. Psychologically speaking, human masculinity can relate to the matrix either as her son or as her lover, but not both at once. That duality of function was and is reserved for the gods. The purpose of the Priapus cycle we have described is to move masculinity from relating to femininity as mother to relating to her as consort. Only in this way can there be a *coniunctio* which will give birth to a viable cultural future.

Of course the question arises: what would a culture be like if masculinity were undivided from *phallos*, uninflated and able to unite creatively with its feminine counterpart?

It is easier to frame such a question than to come up with answers that are not themselves inflated with ingenious fantasy. Nevertheless, it is attractive to speculate that a focus on the *creative* encounter might raise the value of creativity in the culture's eyes. The idea of a culture in which creativity is valued as highly as we presently value inflated masculine pursuits like the accumulation of weapons or wealth certainly provides provocative material with which to fantasize.

But it is more important to think of our present situation. It would not be so terrifying if personal humiliation were the worst possible consequence of our culture's masculine inflation. Unfortunately, technology has arrived at a point at which, used in the service of inflation, it can eliminate our resources for further development in any number of horrifying ways.

Yet can a culture experience and endure humiliation on a profound level, as the myth seems to say it must if *phallos* is to be reintegrated? Recent cultural humiliations that come to mind are Germany after both world wars, the Great Depression and post-Viet Nam America; but they seem to have had little effect on our inflated and destructive uses of technology. A much larger humiliation would seem to be necessary, and it is difficult to imagine what it might be. Worldwide famine or fatal pandemic disease (such as AIDS seems to be) are two possibilities that come to mind, along with the familiar specter of all-out nuclear warfare.

The truth, of course, is that an individual can do nothing to alter a culture directly, for culture changes according to movements in the collective psyche, over which the individual has no control. It has to be enough for an individual to work on his own awareness, for that is truly all one can do. Yet right there, in dealing with the individual psyche, is where many of us miss our opportunities. We cling to our inflated positions as did the man mentioned in the introduction, who managed to avoid discovering his true height for half his lifetime.

Acceptance of height; acceptance, as in Lucius, of baldness; acceptance of asininity, individuality, limitation, aging, infirmity and difference seem to be the simple abilities that *phallos* brings. In contrast, the adolescent appears to need to maintain delusions of perfection and infallibility. Movement from this adolescent position to that of the transformed Lucius would seem a simple thing, and it probably could be so, were the culture not at just the point in its development that it is.

Priapus with snake.
(Roman; Museo Archeological, Verona)

A somewhat similar moment in cultural development appears to have given rise to the myth of Priapus in classical Greece and Rome. It is to be hoped that for us, a general psycho-mythic attitude will appear that serves as well. Jung was not optimistic about the possibility of such a development:

An inflated consciousness is always egocentric and conscious of nothing but its own existence. It is incapable of learning from the past, incapable of understanding contemporary events, and incapable of drawing right conclusions about the future. It is hypnotized by itself and therefore cannot be argued with. It inevitably dooms itself to calamities that must strike it dead. Paradoxically enough, inflation is a regression of consciousness into unconsciousness. This always happens when consciousness takes too many unconscious contents upon itself and loses the faculty of discrimination, the *sine qua non* of all consciousness. When fate, for four whole years, played out a war of monumental frightfulness on the stage of Europe—a war that *nobody* wanted—nobody dreamed of asking exactly who or what had caused the war and its continuation. Nobody realized that European man was possessed by something that robbed him of all free will. And this state of unconscious possession will continue undeterred until we Europeans become scared of our "god-almightiness." Such a change can begin only with individuals . . . . It seems to me of some importance, therefore, that a few individuals, or people individually, should begin to understand that there are contents which do not belong to the ego-personality, but must be ascribed to a psychic non-ego. This mental operation has to be undertaken if we want to avoid a threatening inflation. To help us, we have the useful and edifying models held up to us by poets and philosophers—models or *archetypi* that we may well call remedies for both men and the times. Of course, what we discover there is nothing that can be held up to the masses—only some hidden thing that we can hold up to ourselves in solitude and in silence. [But] it is so much easier to preach the universal panacea to everybody else than to take it oneself, and, as we all know, things are never so bad when everybody is in the same boat. No doubts can exist in the herd; the bigger the crowd the better the truth—and the greater the catastrophe.[2]

---

2 *Psychology and Alchemy*, CW 12, par. 563.

The emergence of elements of the Priapus myth in the dreams of individual men, such as those we have described, suggests that the change in individual awareness to which Jung here refers does have some chance of occurring. To identify it as a salvation, however, would in itself be an inflation. We must simply observe it, "in solitude and in silence," and be aware of what it brings to the individual lives in which it occurs.

Procession of Dionysus.
(from Ovid, *Les Metamorphoses,* trans. l'Abbé Banier, 1732)

Bibliography

Apuleius. *The Golden Ass*. Trans. Robert Graves. New York: Farrar, Strauss, & Giroux, 1951.

_____. *Les Metamorphoses ou l'Asne dor*. Paris: Jean de la Coste, 1648.

Badenoch, Alec W. *Manual of Urology*. 2nd ed. Chicago: Year Book Medical Publishers, Inc., 1974.

Colby, Fletcher H. *Essential Urology*. 2nd ed. Baltimore: Williams & Wilkins, 1953.

Eliade, Mircea. *Rites and Symbols of Initiation*. Trans. Willard R. Trask. New York: Harper & Row, 1975.

Ellenberger, Henri. "The Life and Work of Hermann Rorschach." In *The Bulletin of the Menninger Clinic*, vol. 18, no. 5 (September 1954).

Funk & Wagnalls Standard Dictionary of Folklore, Mythology, and Legend. Ed. Maria Leach. New York: Harper & Row, 1972.

Grant, Michael. *The Art and Life of Pompeii and Herculaneum*. New York: Newsweek, 1979.

Grant, Michael and Mulas, Antonia. *Eros in Pompeii*. New York: Bonanza Books, 1975.

Graves, Robert. *The Greek Myths*. 2 vols. Revised ed. New York: Penguin Books, 1960.

Grayhack, J.T. "Early Shunting Procedures in the Treatment of Priapism." In *Current Controversies in Urologic Management*, ed. Russell Scott Jr. Philadelphia: W. B. Saunders Co., 1972.

Hamilton, William. *Collection of Engravings from Ancient Vases . . . in the Possession of Sir Wm. Hamilton*. Naples: Wm. Tischbein, 1791.

Henderson, Joseph L. *Thresholds of Initiation*. Middletown: Wesleyan University Press, 1967.

Jung, C.G. *The Collected Works* (Bollingen Series XX). 20 vols. Trans. R. F. C. Hull. Ed. H. Head, M. Fordham, G. Adler, Wm. McGuire. Princeton: Princeton University Press, 1953-1979.

Kerényi, C. *The Gods of the Greeks*. Trans. Norman Cameron. London: Thames & Hudson, 1951.

Keuls, Eva. *The Reign of the Phallus*. New York: Harper , 1985.

Knight, Richard Payne. *A Discourse on the Worship of Priapus*. Modern ed. New York: University Books, 1974.

Larousse Encyclopedia of Mythology. Trans. Richard Aldington and Delano Ames. Ed. Felix Guirland. New York: Prometheus Press, 1959.

Lloyd-Jones, Hugh. "Members Only," in *The New York Review*, Nov. 10, 1988.

López-Pedraza, Rafael. *Hermes and His Children*. Zurich: Spring Publications, 1977.

Mann, Thomas. *Death in Venice*. Trans. H.T. Lowe-Porter, New York: Alfred A. Knopf, 1930.

Monick, Eugene. *Phallos: Sacred Image of the Masculine*. Toronto: Inner City Books, 1987.

Otto, W.F. *Dionysus: Myth and Cult*. Bloomington: Indiana University Press, 1965.

Ovid. *Les Metamorphoses*. Trans. l'Abbé Banier. Amsterdam: R. & J. Wetstein & G. Smith, 1732.

Pausanias. *Guide to Greece*. Trans. Peter Levi. Harmondsworth and New York: Penguin Books, 1971.

Petronius. *The Satyricon*. Trans. William Arrowsmith. New York: The New American Library, 1959.

_____. *A Revised Latin Text of the Satyricon*. Illus. Norman Lindsay. London: Ralph Straus, 1890.

Priapeia, The. Trans. Mitchell S. Buck. Privately printed, 1937.

Priapeia: Poems for a Phallic God. Trans. W.H. Parker. London: Croom Helm, 1988.

Richlin, Amy. *The Garden of Priapus*. New Haven: Yale University Press, 1982.

Rorschach, Hermann. *Gesammelte Aufsätze*. Bern and Stuttgart: Verlag Hans Huber, 1965.

Sharp, Daryl. *The Survival Papers: Anatomy of a Midlife Crisis*. Toronto: Inner City Books, 1988.

St. Evremont, Mons. *The Satyrical Works of Titus Petronius Arbiter*. London: Sam. Briscoe, 1708.

Stedman's Medical Dictionary. 23rd ed. Baltimore: Williams & Wilkins, 1976.

Symeoni, M. Gabriello. *La Vita et Metamorfoses d'Ovidio.* Lione: Giovanni de Torres, 1559.

Trip, Edward. *The Meridian Handbook of Classical Mythology.* New York: Meridian, 1970.

Vanggaard, Thorkil. *Phallos: A Symbol and Its History in the Male World.* New York: International Universities Press, 1972.

Von Franz, Marie-Louise. *A Psychological Interpretation of the Golden Ass of Apuleius.* 2nd ed. Dallas: Spring Publications, 1980.

Whitmont, Edward C. *Return of the Goddess.* New York: Crossroad, 1984.

Winter, C.C. "The Nonoperative Management of Priapism." In *Current Controversies in Urologic Management,* ed. Russell Scott Jr. Philadelphia: W.B. Saunders Co, 1972.

Index

Numbers in italics refer to illustrations

122

Addiction to Perfection
The Still Unravished Bride

A Psychological Study by
Marion Woodman

12. Addiction to Perfection: The Still Unravished Bride.
Marion Woodman (Toronto). ISBN 0-919123-11-2. 208 pp. $15

"This book is about taking the head off an evil witch." With these words Marion Woodman begins her spiral journey, a powerful and authoritative look at the psychology and attitudes of modern woman.

The witch is a Medusa or a Lady Macbeth, an archetypal pattern functioning autonomously in women, petrifying their spirit and inhibiting their development as free and creatively receptive individuals. Much of this, according to the author, is due to a cultural one-sidedness that favors patriarchal values—productivity, goal orientation, intellectual excellence, spiritual perfection, etc.—at the expense of more earthy, interpersonal values that have traditionally been recognized as the heart of the feminine.

Marion Woodman's first book, *The Owl Was a Baker's Daughter: Obesity, Anorexia Nervosa and the Repressed Feminine,* focused on the psychology of eating disorders and weight disturbances.

Here, with a broader perspective on the same general themes, she continues her remarkable exploration of women's mysteries through case material, dreams, literature and mythology, in food rituals, rape symbolism, Christianity, imagery in the body, sexuality, creativity and relationships.

"It is like finding the loose end in a knotted mass of thread. . . . What a relief! Somebody knows!"—**Elizabeth Strahan,** *Psychological Perspectives.*

Studies in Jungian Psychology
by Jungian Analysts

Limited Edition Paperbacks

Prices and payment in U.S. dollars (except for Canadian orders)

1. The Secret Raven: Conflict and Transformation.
Daryl Sharp (Toronto). ISBN 0-919123-00-7. 128 pp. $13
A practical study of *puer* psychology, including dream interpretation and material on midlife crisis, the provisional life, the mother complex, anima and shadow. Illustrated.

2. The Psychological Meaning of Redemption Motifs in Fairytales.
Marie-Louise von Franz (Zurich). ISBN 0-919123-01-5. 128 pp. $13
Unique approach to understanding typical dream motifs (bathing, clothes, animals, etc.).

3. On Divination and Synchronicity: The Psychology of Meaningful Chance.
Marie-Louise von Franz (Zurich). ISBN 0-919123-02-3. 128 pp. $13
Penetrating study of irrational methods of divining fate (I Ching, astrology, palmistry, Tarot cards, etc.), contrasting Western ideas with those of so-called primitives. Illustrated.

4. The Owl Was a Baker's Daughter: Obesity, Anorexia and the Repressed Feminine. Marion Woodman (Toronto). ISBN 0-919123-03-1. 144 pp. $14
A modern classic, with particular attention to the body as mirror of the psyche in weight disturbances and eating disorders. Based on case studies, dreams and mythology. Illus.

5. Alchemy: An Introduction to the Symbolism and the Psychology.
Marie-Louise von Franz (Zurich). ISBN 0-919123-04-X. 288 pp. $18
Detailed guide to what the alchemists were really looking for: emotional wholeness. Invaluable for interpreting images and motifs in modern dreams and drawings. **84 illustrations.**

6. Descent to the Goddess: A Way of Initiation for Women.
Sylvia Brinton Perera (New York). ISBN 0-919123-05-8. 112 pp. $12
A timely and provocative study of the need for an inner, female authority in a masculine-oriented society. Rich in insights from mythology and the author's analytic practice.

7. The Psyche as Sacrament: C.G. Jung and Paul Tillich.
John P. Dourley (Ottawa). ISBN 0-919123-06-6. 128 pp. $13
Comparative study from a dual perspective (author is Catholic priest and Jungian analyst), exploring the psychological meaning of religion, God, Christ, the spirit, the Trinity, etc.

8. Border Crossings: Carlos Castaneda's Path of Knowledge.
Donald Lee Williams (Boulder). ISBN 0-919123-07-4. 160 pp. $14
The first thorough psychological examination of the Don Juan novels, bringing Castaneda's spiritual journey down to earth. Special attention to the psychology of the feminine.

9. Narcissism and Character Transformation. The Psychology of Narcissistic Character Disorders. ISBN 0-919123-08-2. 192 pp. $15
Nathan Schwartz-Salant (New York).
A comprehensive study of narcissistic character disorders, drawing upon a variety of analytic points of view (Jung, Freud, Kohut, Klein, etc.). Theory and clinical material. Illus.

10. Rape and Ritual: A Psychological Study.
Bradley A. Te Paske (Minneapolis). ISBN 0-919123-09-0. 160 pp. $14
Incisive combination of theory, clinical material and mythology. Illustrated.

11. Alcoholism and Women: The Background and the Psychology.
Jan Bauer (Montreal). ISBN 0-919123-10-4. 144 pp. $14
Sociology, case material, dream analysis and archetypal patterns from mythology.

12. Addiction to Perfection: The Still Unravished Bride.
Marion Woodman (Toronto). ISBN 0-919123-11-2. 208 pp. $15
A powerful and authoritative look at the psychology of modern women. Examines dreams, mythology, food rituals, body imagery, sexuality and creativity. A continuing best-seller since its original publication in 1982. Illustrated.

13. Jungian Dream Interpretation: A Handbook of Theory and Practice.
James A. Hall, M.D. (Dallas). ISBN 0-919123-12-0. 128 pp. $13
A practical guide, including common dream motifs and many clinical examples.

14. The Creation of Consciousness: Jung's Myth for Modern Man.
Edward F. Edinger, M.D. (Los Angeles). ISBN 0-919123-13-9. 128 pp. $13
Insightful study of the meaning and purpose of human life. Illustrated.

15. The Analytic Encounter: Transference and Human Relationship.
Mario Jacoby (Zurich). ISBN 0-919123-14-7. 128 pp. $13
Sensitive exploration of the difference between relationships based on projection and I-Thou relationships characterized by mutual respect and psychological objectivity.

16. Change of Life: Psychological Study of Dreams and the Menopause.
Ann Mankowitz (Santa Fe). ISBN 0-919123-15-5. 128 pp. $13
A moving account of an older woman's Jungian analysis, dramatically revealing the later years as a time of rebirth, a unique opportunity for psychological development.

17. The Illness That We Are: A Jungian Critique of Christianity.
John P. Dourley (Ottawa). ISBN 0-919123-16-3. 128 pp. $13
Radical study by Catholic priest and analyst, exploring Jung's qualified appreciation of Christian symbols and ritual, while questioning the masculine ideals of Christianity.

18. Hags and Heroes: A Feminist Approach to Jungian Therapy with Couples.
Polly Young-Eisendrath (Philadelphia). ISBN 0-919123-17-1. 192 pp. $15
Highly original integration of feminist views with the concepts of Jung and Harry Stack Sullivan. Detailed strategies and techniques, emphasis on feminine authority.

19. Cultural Attitudes in Psychological Perspective.
Joseph Henderson , M.D. (San Francisco). ISBN 0-919123-18-X. 128 pp. $13
Shows how a psychological attitude can give depth to one's world view. Illustrated.

20. The Vertical Labyrinth: Individuation in Jungian Psychology.
Aldo Carotenuto (Rome). ISBN 0-919123-19-8. 144 pp. $14
A guided journey through the world of dreams and psychic reality, illustrating the process of individual psychological development.

21. The Pregnant Virgin: A Process of Psychological Transformation.
Marion Woodman (Toronto). ISBN 0-919123-20-1. 208 pp. $16
A celebration of the feminine, in both men and women. Explores the wisdom of the body, eating disorders, relationships, dreams, addictions, etc. Illustrated.

22. Encounter with the Self: William Blake's *Illustrations of the Book of Job.*
Edward F. Edinger, M.D. (Los Angeles). ISBN 0-919123-21-X. 80 pp. $10
Penetrating commentary on the Biblical Job story as a numinous, archetypal event. Complete with Blake's original 22 engravings.

23. The Scapegoat Complex: Toward a Mythology of Shadow and Guilt.
Sylvia Brinton Perera (New York). ISBN 0-919123-22-8. 128 pp. $13
A hard-hitting study of victim psychology in modern men and women, based on case material, mythology and archetypal patterns.

24. The Bible and the Psyche: Individuation Symbolism in the Old Testament.
Edward F. Edinger (Los Angeles). ISBN 0-919123-23-6. 176 pp. $15
A major new work relating significant Biblical events to the psychological movement toward wholeness that takes place in individuals.

25. The Spiral Way: A Woman's Healing Journey.
Aldo Carotenuto (Rome). ISBN 0-919123-24-4. 144 pp. $14
Detailed case history of a fifty-year-old woman's Jungian analysis, with particular attention to her dreams and the rediscovery of her enthusiasm for life.

26. The Jungian Experience: Analysis and Individuation.
James A. Hall, M.D. (Dallas). ISBN 0-919123-25-2. 176 pp. $15
Comprehensive study of the theory and clinical application of Jungian thought, including Jung's model, the structure of analysis, where to find an analyst, training centers, etc.

27. Phallos: Sacred Image of the Masculine.
Eugene Monick (Scranton/New York). ISBN 0-919123-26-0. 144 pp. $14
Uncovers the essence of masculinity (as opposed to the patriarchy) through close examination of the physical, mythological and psychological aspects of phallos. **30 illustrations.**

28. The Christian Archetype: A Jungian Commentary on the Life of Christ.
Edward F. Edinger, M.D. (Los Angeles). ISBN 0-919123-27-9. 144 pp. $14
Psychological view of images and events central to the Christian myth, showing their symbolic meaning in terms of personal individuation. **31 illustrations.**

29. Love, Celibacy and the Inner Marriage.
John P. Dourley (Ottawa). ISBN 0-919123-28-7. 128 pp. $13
Shows that without a deeply compassionate relationship to the inner anima/animus, we cannot relate to our intimates or to God, to the full depth of our ability to love.

30. Touching: Body Therapy and Depth Psychology.
Deldon Anne McNeely (Lynchburg, VA). ISBN 0-919123-29-5. 128 pp. $13
Illustrates how these two disciplines, both concerned with restoring life to an ailing human psyche, may be integrated in theory and practice. Focus on the healing power of touch.

31. Personality Types: Jung's Model of Typology.
Daryl Sharp (Toronto). ISBN 0-919123-30-9. 128 pp. $13
Detailed explanation of Jung's model (basis for the widely-used Myers-Briggs Type Indicator), showing its implications for individual development and for relationships. Illus.

32. The Sacred Prostitute: Eternal Aspect of the Feminine.
Nancy Qualls-Corbett (Birmingham). ISBN 0-919123-31-7. 176 pp. $15
Shows how our vitality and capacity for joy depend on rediscovering the ancient connection between spirituality and passionate love. Illustrated. **(Foreword by Marion Woodman.)**

33. When the Spirits Come Back.
Janet O. Dallett (Seal Harbor, WA). ISBN 0-919123-32-5. 160 pp. $14
An analyst examines herself, her profession and the limitations of prevailing attitudes toward mental disturbance. Interweaving her own story with descriptions of those who come to her for help, she details her rediscovery of the integrity of the healing process.

34. The Mother: Archetypal Image in Fairy Tales.
Sibylle Birkhäuser-Oeri (Zurich). ISBN 0-919123-33-3. 176 pp. $15
Compares processes in the unconscious with common images and motifs in folk-lore. Illustrates how positive and negative mother complexes affect us all, with examples from many well-known fairy tales and daily life. **(Edited by Marie-Louise von Franz.)**

35. The Survival Papers: Anatomy of a Midlife Crisis.
Daryl Sharp (Toronto). ISBN 0-919123-34-1. 160 pp. $15
Jung's major concepts—persona, shadow, anima and animus, complexes, projection, typology, active imagination, individuation, etc.—are dramatically presented in the immediate context of an analysand's process. And the analyst's.

36. The Cassandra Complex: Living with Disbelief.
Laurie Layton Schapira (New York). ISBN 0-919123-35-X. 160 pp. $15
Shows how unconscious, prophetic sensibilities can be transformed from a burden into a valuable source of conscious understanding. Includes clinical material and an examination of the role of powerfully intuitive, medial women through history. Illustrated.

37. Dear Gladys: The Survival Papers, Book 2
Daryl Sharp (Toronto). ISBN 0-919123-36-8. 144 pp. $15
An entertaining and instructive continuation of the story begun in *The Survival Papers* (title 35). Part textbook, part novel, part personal exposition.

Prices and payment (check or money order) in $U.S. (in Canada, $Cdn)

Please add $1 per book (bookpost) or $3 per book (airmail)

INNER CITY BOOKS
Box 1271, Station Q, Toronto, Canada M4T 2P4